GEORG KÜHLEWIND

FEELING KNOWING

COLLECTED ESSAYS

TRANSLATED AND EDITED
BY
FRIEDEMANN SCHWARZKOPF

RUDOLF STEINER COLLEGE PRESS

Rudolf Steiner College Press
9200 Fair Oaks Boulevard
Fair Oaks, California 95628
U.S.A.
(916) 961 8729

Cover Drawing: Denis Klocek

Peaceful Valley Farm
20465 Placer Hills Road
Colfax, California 95713
U.S.A.

ACKNOWLEDGEMENTS

We would like to thank:
The *Journal for Anthroposophy* for the kind permission to reprint some previously published articles;
Ginette Bell and Lynnae LeBlanc for editing.

CONTENTS

TRANSLATOR'S PREFACE

The main purpose of this collection is to make available to the interested reader some recent essays by Georg Kühlewind. Several of these were published in different issues of the *Journal for Anthroposophy*, others have not been published before. All of them were originally written in German, and most of them have been published in German-language newsletters etc. Since it is difficult for the English speaking reader to trace them, and since it may take some years before they can be published in English in the context of the books for which Kühlewind originally wrote them, Rudolf Steiner College Press is presenting them here in a third of a series of similar volumes. A list of other books published in English is enclosed at the end of this collection.

Therefore the essays published here have to be read as independent studies on specific subjects within the context of Anthroposophy, spiritual scientific, philosophical research, and schooling of consciousness. They provide little "information," but ask us to practice a contemplative reading where we actualize the thinking — respectively feeling gesture from where these texts are written — in such a way that we can verify the reality of these observations in our own experience.

We entitled this collection as "Feeling Knowing," because it illustrates, characterizes and describes a way of knowing — by way concepts which can guide our thought to this higher feeling — which may be also be called "cognizing feeling." Already in Rudolf Steiner College Press's first volume of this series, *Schooling of Consciousness,* an essay entitled "The Second Stage of Meditation," emphasizes the difference between a so-called "self-feeling," and a self-less "knowing feeling" that is not interested in how something makes *us* feel, but how something reveals its inner nature when we reverse our feeling will to the "other" (ideal or sense-perceptual phenomenon), such that it can reveal itself to us through our reversed feeling will. In this way our feeling attention is no longer pointing to ourselves, but increasingly surrendered to the other.

This can be considered as the thread that connects the essays published in this volume: the feeling knowing in artistic activity, in perception of Nature, in the cognitive experience of philosophical works and meditative texts, and in the "feeling of evidence" at the root of every moral-ethical and scientific judgment. In all cases the Logos-nature of the practicing reader is addressed by the initial Logos of the phenomenon, until they merge in the communion of silent unison.

September 1993

Friedemann Schwarzkopf

SOURCES

ART AND COGNITION
Translation: Friedemann Schwarzkopf. 1993. From unpublished essay:
Kühlewind, Georg: "Kunst und Erkennen."

LANGUAGE AND MUSIC
Translation: Friedemann Schwarzkopf. 1988. Rev. 1991, 1992. From unpublished essay:
Kühlewind, Georg. "Sprache und Musik." 1988.

PERCEPTION EXERCISES
Translation: Friedemann Schwarzkopf. 1989. From:
Kühlewind., Georg. *Die Wiederbelebung der Sinne — Wege zum fühlenden Wahrnehmen*. Chapter 8: "Wahrnehmungsübungen." Stuttgart, Germany: Verlag Freies Geistesleben. 1989.

FROM EPIPHANY TO EASTER
Translation from German manuscript: Friedemann Schwarzkopf;
Kühlewind, Georg. "Von Epiphania zu Ostern." *Das Goetheanum — Wochenschrift für Anthroposophie*. No. 12. 24. März 1991. pp.105-108
Kühlewind, Georg. *Journal for Anthroposophy*. "From Epiphany to Easter." No 56, Spring 1993, pp. 72-82.

WHITSUN
Translation: Friedemann Schwarzkopf, edited by Maria St. Goar and Linda Fleishman, from
Kühlewind, Georg. "Pfingsten." *Das Goetheanum — Wochenschrift für Anthroposophie*. 66. Jahrgang, Nr. 24. 7. Juni 1987.
Kühlewind, Georg. *Journal for Anthroposophy*. "Whitsun." No. 49, Summer 1989, pp. 21-28.

FROM WHITSUN TO MICHAELMAS
Translation: Friedemann Schwarzkopf, 2.Dec.1992. from:
Kühlewind, Georg. "Von Pfingsten zu Michaeli." *Das Goetheanum — Wochenschrift für Anthroposophie*. Nr. 22. 30. Mai 1993, pp. 225-227

CHRIST AND MICHAEL
Translation: Friedemann Schwarzkopf. 16. Apr. 93. From:
Kühlewind, Georg. "Christus und Michael." *Das Goetheanum — Wochenschrift für Anthroposophie*. No. 39. 27 September 1992.

THE SUBSTANCE OF THE I

Translation: Friedemann Schwarzkopf. 1986. From:
Kühlewind, Georg. *Die Substanz des Ich*. unpublished German Manuscript.

THE FORCE OF THE LOGOS AND THE FORCE OF THE "I"

Translation: Friedemann Schwarzkopf. 1989. from German manuscript:
Kühlewind. Georg. *Logoskraft und Ichkraft*.
Kühlewind. Georg. *Journal for Anthroposophy*. Fall 1990 No. 51, pp. 70-79 and Spring 1991 No. 52, pp. 46-57.

LOVE AND FEAR

Translation: Friedemann Schwarzkopf. From unpublished German manuscript.
Kühlewind, Georg. "Liebe und Furcht"
Kühlewind, Georg. "Love and Fear." *Journal for Anthroposophy*. Fall 1992 No. 55, pp. 62-68.

THE SUPRA-NATIONAL FACULTIES OF THE HUMAN BEING

Translation: Friedemann Schwarzkopf. 24.VIII.1992 From:
Kühlewind, Georg. "Die Übernationalen Fähigkeiten des Menschen." *Das Goetheanum — Wochenschrift für Anthroposophie*. Nr. 19, 10. Mai 1992, pp. 199-201.

BEHOLD, I MAKE EVERYTHING ANEW

Translation: Friedemann Schwarzkopf. From:
Kühlewind, Georg., "Siehe, ich mache alles neu." *Das Goetheanum — Wochenschrift für Anthroposophie*. 66. Jahrgang Nr. 22, 24. Mai 1987.

THEORIES OF CONSCIOUSNESS

Lecture Tuesday, April 22, 1986, 8.00 P.M.
University of California Los Angeles (UCLA)
Sponsor: International College, Los Angeles.
Transcript: Susan McManamon, Edited by Friedemann Schwarzkopf.

ART AND COGNITION

1.

At first the two spiritual phenomena of art and cognition seem easily distinguishable. Cognition happens in the inner, soul-spiritual sphere; art always has to appear in the sense perceptual world, requiring material substance to become sense-perceptible. The manifestation of cognition—or its roots—is aesthetically modest. Cognition does not need to be expressed; the way and manner in which it appears is secondary; expression happens *after* the cognitive act. For art, sense-perceptual appearance is essential; there is nothing before it appears; this "appearing" can also happen in imagination (as image, poem or music), but then it is fashioned after the model of sense-perceptual material experience.

In this respect art is analogous to language. Like language it has two aspects: the inner side is the *meaning* or *sense* which appears outwardly as acoustic or optical phenomenon — with the difference that the "inner side" of a phenomenon of art is precisely not merely a thought entity: otherwise art would be superfluous.

The *form* in which the artistic phenomenon appears must also satisfy the criterion of beauty. In art, beauty is always in the perceptual sphere, although one also speaks about the "beauty" of a demonstration in mathematics or logic; there is even a prize on the beauty of a chess game. But these "beauties" don't appear to the senses, and they have nothing to do with beauty in art, they belong to the sphere of cognition.

But common to art and cognition is the creative element. Both art and cognition give something new to their creator — and ideally to all human beings: One can feel their common root. We have to examine how they unfold.[1]

We owe it to this common source that—in art and cognition—meaning, sense, and "wording" can spiritually appear: in other words, their logos- or idea-nature. The origin of Ideas lies in infinite heights from where they gradually descend. If we can be satisfied with three steps of the heavenly ladder (and for our purposes, that is enough), we can discover a kind of will in every idea and in every thought — they *will* to be this specific idea. When a new thought is dawning it is initially this kind of will which surfaces like a

---

* From: Kühlewind. Georg: "Kunst und Erkennen." Unpublished essay. Translation: Friedemann Schwarzkopf. 1993.

[1] Even though art gives us many insights as we learn to produce and practice it, this is not its ultimate aim. Art wants to imbue the perceptual world with "sense."

gentle ripple on the blue sky of the elevated consciousness. Then a kind of feeling emerges from this will, just a little more specific than the ripples of will. And from the feeling proceeds a living stream of thinking, already more distinct, yet still without language, without words. But later this fluid medium will coagulate into more or less consistent thoughts and crystallize into words. These are meaningful only for a listener or recipient who allows them to resurrect.

The birth of an artistic idea happens similarly; the first two stages are identical. However, once the cloud of feeling has formed, the artistic phenomenon is immediately produced; living thinking and the level of thought are avoided. Because if the idea has become concrete enough to appear in the form of living thinking—still suitable for a manifoldness of expression—it can no longer become a genuine and good piece of art; for that purpose it would have to remain in the sphere of feeling ("objective" feeling, see below). Art always manifests a form of feeling in the sense-perceptual world.

2.

If the art product could be replaced by thoughts, or if it would require a conceptual explanation (for instance, program music which would be indigestible without knowledge of the program), it would not be art,[2] because art speaks to the child in the human being which perceives the world in a feeling-willing willing-feeling (with a "reversed" will, coming from the perceived object, thereby modeling our receptive will and attention). This retroactive aspect shows itself in the artistic behavior of the senses, where we never find just one single sense in activity, but practically ***all*** the senses. Therefore, in characterizing artistic activities. one speaks about "balance," "movement," "warm colors," "hard sound," etc. One can say that art is a sphere where we can still perceive in a feeling way, like children — of course, this illustrates only ***one*** aspect of the artistic consciousness, because the contents and qualities of feeling in the arts are not at all simple. In Nature, we reject the willing "feelable" ideas, because they are too mighty and unbearable for us. We quickly cover the perception with concepts, dead concepts—not permeated by life—which neutralize and kill what meets us in Nature.

[2] Today, in many spheres of art, one believes that one can produce art without the idea of beauty. There are "interesting," "unusual," "stimulating" art creations. Mostly they need a thought explanation, or they try to stimulate reflection. One can often admire an ingenious originality. But it is questionable whether this is a misunderstanding of the category of "art".

In art we deal with forms and ideas of feeling, which do not speak to our subjective feelings and emotions (even though this is what happens easily) but address our cognizing, "objective," communicative feeling, which is comparable to our shared communicative-universal element of thinking. One can also perceive art without the normal kind of concepts — thinking is dissolved within the cognizing "intelligent" feeling, not separate from it.

"Feelable ideas" are much larger than "living ideas." This is why it is possible to paint a landscape in various ways "beautifully," to play a piece of music in many ways "beautifully." "Beauty" is an intuition, an experience; like "truth," "goodness" or any other fundamental idea, beauty cannot be realized on the consciousness-level of past (discursive) thought.

In the same way as the universal nature of thinking, communicative feeling comes to appearance in human beings.

Hence, the pedagogy of art has two aims: on the one hand to educate the specific ***feeling sensitivity*** which is characteristic for the perceptual field of the art-form; on the other hand, teach the ***technique*** of the art-form for the necessary interaction with its material medium (instrument, brush and paint, clay and stone, one's own body, etc.), so that the hand—and through the hand the whole body—can become a ***speech organ***. This standard means that one has to educate an ***intelligent "seeing" will***, which finds its aims, goals and forms of movement not from thought representational mental pictures, but carries the "what" of its will within itself. In essence, artistic "technique" means this kind of seeing ***will*** in the respective medium.[3]

3.

In earlier periods of art-history, the themes were ***feelable***; therefore they could inspire the artistic activity. The image of a "Madonna with the Child" could kindle the religious feeling—at least for moments of deep contemplation—and supply the image as well as the painter with a foundation in feeling; a landscape or a face can have the same effect. When the feeling quality began to disappear in perceiving, mental picturing and also in the religious life, the theme became more and more a pretext to use sensory elements

[3] For instance, when we are speaking we are not controlling our speech organs by way of mental picturing or thinking; this would be impossible; we are not even concerned what our speech-organs are doing. This is not merely the effect of earlier instruction—because even the little child does not know what the speech-organs have to do to reproduce something it has heard—this is the type of superconscious activity of the will which is the purpose of artistic pedagogy.

which could still *embody* and emanate feeling; the theme no longer inspired feeling. At the root of all sensory qualities is the primal or all-encompassing sense: the knowing feeling. In the small child, this primal sense is still alive, its perceiving is a global perception, the single senses are working together, not yet separately, and feeling is the fundamental experience in perception. This feeling—experiencing as well as engendering the act of perception—reappears in art as *beauty*.

More recently, this pretext has been abandoned and now one works with the *elements* of the respective art-form. This attempt is less successful in those arts which work with the element of speech: there, the *tie* between the theme and the form of expression is very close; at the same time, the theme can be dealt with on several levels because of the vertical manifoldness-of-meaning of the words.[4]

4.

When we compare Nature and art, we find that both are experienced by way of sense-perception. Both display feeling and willing; in fact, they consist of feeling and will, except that art is like a piece of Nature that is touched and tamed by the human hand, brought closer to the human being.

> ...the beautiful is only
> the birth of the fright which we can barely endure;
> and we admire it so much because it calmly abstains
> to destroy us.

This is how the poet Rilke depicts his aesthetics in the first of his *Duino Elegies*. In the second elegy it says:

> Where are the days of Tobias,
> when one of the most radiant ones stood before the simple entrance of the house
> a little disguised for the journey and no longer frightening.

As the archangel makes Himself bearable for the human being when He is "a little disguised," so is Nature in art. None of the elements of speech—sounds, grammar and syntax—nor the elements of art have their origin in Nature. In Nature one finds no pure musical tone (not even in the song of birds), no color-composition like a painted picture (even naturalism has not succeeded, and where it seems to succeed, the question arises whether it is still art or a peculiar transition to imitation of Nature). No phenomenon of

[4] The "vertical manifoldness" is easiest to experience in the symbolic language of myths and fairy tales. As image, an object or being has many meanings which cannot be expressed in other ways. This aspect of words is also applied in demanding or meditative texts.

Nature can be seen in the way in which an image or sculpture allows it to appear: both still and in motion at the same time etc.

Art is not "given": it is a creation of human beings. Through art, new forms of feeling are created; the artist is inspired by a new feeling *and* expresses it in the perceptual world; "and" means that this is a simultaneous event.

The evolution of consciousness of mankind (and the child also develops on those lines) leads from *saturated* perception to self-consciousness, and when self-consciousness is reached, perceiving and thinking can be intensified further. Perception is "saturated" when the Idea enters the consciousness not only through thought (or its precursor), but is also contained in perception. The inner space, where thinking can live independently of perception, develops at a later stage. Self-consciousness arises after thinking has emancipated itself from knowing feeling and willing, and when—at the stage of the consciousness-soul—a soul-spiritual structure is formed which makes reflection possible: at that stage awareness is predominantly on the level of the past (finished, pictured thought etc.). But in every *new* understanding, awareness can *touch* the level of Truth, of Living Thinking: on the plane of Imagination. And there, perception can be enlivened through *exercises*,[5] with a simultaneous raising of the level of our inner—spiritual—activity; the lowest level of this spiritual activity is called "Thinking."[*] And in the beholding of the *archetypal phenomenon* perceiving and thinking understanding coincide in a similar way as in the perception of art: in both cases the perceived is "read" (in a similar way as in hearing when the *sense* of a text also has to be read by melting the words into a unity of meaning).

Several decades ago, science and art worked in a more or less superconscious connection with the source of ideas (also artistic ideas). We have to be prepared that this access—like everything that is given—will become increasingly difficult or end altogether. Science has been established on a level of consciousness where it cannot be adequate to the reality of Nature and the human being. Therefore it is necessary to develop a meditative science.

The way would be to try to extend our momentary lightening-like connection with the level where *understanding* takes place, in inner presence, which happens in every *new* understanding. We have to learn to articulate on this higher plane. And in order to

---

[5] Kühlewind, Georg. ***From Normal to Healthy***. Chapter 5 "The Path of Knowledge". Lindisfarne Press, Hudson, NY. 1993.
Kühlewind, Georg. ***Freiheit Erüben***. Chapter "Schulung der Aufmerksamkeit", Stuttgart, Germany: Verlag Freies Geistesleben. 1988. Kühlewind, Georg. ***Die Belehrung der Sinne — Wege zur fühlenden Wahrnehmung***. Stuttgart, Germany: Verlag Freies Geistesleben. 1990.

[*] the activity which produces thought.. (note by translator)

strengthen and increase this connection we have to practice—by way of consciousness-exercises—wordless thinking and perceiving. Later we will be able to extend this to higher levels of consciousness.

A ***scientific, researching meditation*** begins by bringing the theme (i.e., the question or problem) into a form which can be suitable for meditation. This can be the form of a sentence or image. For the more advanced, it can also be a situation, a barely formulated question, a kind of "what is that?" or only a "how?" The researcher concentrates on the theme, i.e. the ***meaning*** of the sentence independently of the words in which it is articulated, or the question in the form of an image,[6] until the theme becomes transparent and the attention shifts into a receptive gesture. The theme then dissolves in living thinking, which is always accompanied by feeling. And as the thinking becomes transparent, and as the attention shifts into feeling, the next step is to ***renounce*** the clearly identified, fluid, living thought-element which was elaborated in the beginning. If one can articulate within the feeling of the theme (which normally happens in moments of living thinking), one identifies within the activity of feeling a rather cloud-like characteristic ***form of feeling***, through an attention which does not yet think or perceive, but ***feel.***

The following stage demands another renunciation, namely a renunciation of the attained quality of feeling. By concentrating on feeling, the form of feeling can go through a new metamorphosis. The feeling fades as it turns into a kind of will, and our attention changes accordingly from a feeling to a willing attention. Now our attention faces a still more general formation, less "defined" in the ordinary sense, yet entirely specific in a higher sense, simply a form of will.

For example, one can think of the only moral intuition in the New Testament: "Love one another as I have loved you;" this intuition lives on the level of the will, and in order to manifest it on the earth it has to undergo several metamorphoses—again by ever new intuitions—into feeling, into living thinking and down to the everyday-consciousness to be applicable to the individual case.

This descending ("bringing down") is equally as difficult as the rising and has to be learned. In ascending one encounters something new at every level, and the experience of a higher plane does not simply "correspond" to what was established on a lower plane,

[6] Kühlewind, Georg. ***From Normal to Healthy***. Chapter 5 "The Path of Knowledge". Lindisfarne Press, Hudson, NY. 1993.
Kühlewind, Georg. ***Freiheit Erüben***. Chapter "Schulung der Aufmerksamkeit", Stuttgart, Germany: Verlag Freies Geistesleben. 1988. Kühlewind, Georg. ***Die Belehrung der Sinne — Wege zur fühlenden Wahrnehmung***. Stuttgart, Germany: Verlag Freies Geistesleben. 1990.

but always adds something. If one reaches the cognition of will, this experience renders something different in comparison to the experience of the feeling which was experienced in rising. When one wants to bring the intuition "down" as cognition, one must not be impatient, not bring it too quickly to the level of the text; if that happens, the sense can be distorted or entirely lost.

Patiently one seeks the new feeling at the place where the flow of thinking springs forth, and in the end one allows the verbal formulation to be stimulated by ever-new feeling inspiration for the appropriate words as a meditative text. Spiritual experiences can only be rendered as approximation through a meditative sign-language (text, image, ritual).

If the motive for meditation is not research but search for ***artistic inspiration***, the ladder of ascent proceeds in the same way as in the cognitive meditation. Today this can be recommended for a schooling of consciousness (because the faculties we bring with us into life are faculties we have not consciously acquired; they fade around the middle of our lives). However, the meditant should feel an anticipating kinship to the inner feeling (but this applies also to the cognitive meditation).

The descending path divides in the field of cognitive feeling. Because in the artistic meditation actual ***doing*** should begin at this level. The feeling meditation should not descend any further into the flow of thinking, but seize and steer the artistic intelligent will. As one can consider the formation of natural objects as a process where a higher will inserted itself into the sensorially perceptible substantiality, one can consider art as something which comes into being through a human will which is guided by feeling inspiration, thus molding the substantiality in an intelligent way.

To enable the artistic will to obey the inspiration, the body and especially the involved organs and limbs have to become a ***speech-organ*** in order to "utter" what the inspiration wants to express. This requires a dual preparation: knowledge of the medium (instrument, color, tone, etc.) and union with the theme, the predominant or primary sense (the sense of sight in painting, the sense of hearing in music, sensing-touching in sculpture etc.). In the artistic sphere the primary sense works both actively and passively, at the same time giving and receiving, as in speech where active and passive converge in articulating and perceiving one's own articulation.

In perceiving, the senses are usually passive, working receptively. The sense of balance and the sense of life are an exception because they make simultaneous adjustments in the bodily organism when they notice an uncomfortable or painful position (stumbling, tiredness). But the clearest exception is the sense of movement which coordinates our movements—since earliest childhood—like an "artist," especially in walking and speaking: this sense directs and perceives our movements ***from within*** (it is not necessary to observe the hands to know what one is doing). In artistic activity the sense of movement is subordinated to the predominant primary sense (in painting, for instance, to the sense of sight). Thus it is the specific artistic sensitivity (e.g. hearing in music) which controls movement. Practice and exercise, for instance at the musical instrument, have the same function for the sense of movement as continued speaking and hearing of words for the sense of speech.

Knowledge of the artistic medium means to unite the sense-organism—especially the sense of movement—with the tool or the instrument (in many arts the instrument is one's own body). This growing-together means that the sense of touch and the sense of movement are extended into the instrument through feeling: a "feeling" of the piano's entire mechanism, the brush, the paint, the friction of the hair of the violin bow, etc. The instrument itself becomes a sense-organ, an organ of movement. The activity is entirely permeated with feeling, feeling which integrates the instrument: this guarantees that the activity is artistic, i.e. that it ***speaks***.[7]

In cognitive meditation the insight becomes tangible through the gradual descent, the leap from the living stream of thinking to articulated thought. In ***art*** this corresponds to the transition from the form of feeling to the sense-perceptual sphere. The resulting perception remains ambiguous, with many meanings, like a meditative text.

In ***feeling***, the way begins with the predominant or primary sense of the respective artistic discipline, while all other senses are covibrating. This sense is actively molding the appearing "picture" (or acoustical image) which will ultimately affect the perceiver through his receptive will. Simultaneously or later (as for instance in a stage play) the perceptual image is grasped by the predominant sense: the other senses are covibrating. Then the sensory activity is stirring and forming the feeling. The image which emerges in this way (in the actual artistic process) becomes the theme for the sense of movement, which is simultaneously—actively and passively—realizing the image: ***this*** image did not exist before. The predominant primary sense ***and*** the sense of movement produce the image. One could say that the dominant sense inspires the sense of movement. All of this happens simultaneously, in inner presence, on the level where living thinking takes place, the plane of Imagination.

[7] To write poetry and prose means to work with qualities of sound, or imaginations of sound, because silent reading of artistic texts requires at least the inner imagination of how it would sound. Until the fourth century the only way to read was to read out loud.

In essence, feeling happens *above* sense-perception, although the senses originate in feeling and can also resurface as feeling, for instance when they are activated in artistic practice where we were able to identify their retroactive nature. This makes it possible to practice art and to experience it simultaneously. In the inner sphere of the soul—where the supersensible thinking happens independently of perceptual counterparts—living thinking surveys the activity of feeling. Through the senses the control finally leads to the sense of movement, and through it to the perceptual world.

Art transforms the sense-perceptual world. Cognition—by itself—does not change the world until its conclusions are outwardly applied. This application can *create* meaning. Yet it can also be meaningless: this happens in all transformations of the sense-perceptual world for egoistic motives — also in the global humanitarian sphere. Technical inventions which serve the egoity also belong to this field, such as comfort or the secondary human instincts which do not "speak," which means that they have not come about in order to communicate something.

The *meaningless* enters the world through the human being. However, the human being can later supply such meaning through integration into the service of a *meaningful*, meaning-creating life.

Art transforms the sense-perceptual world in a "speaking" manner, creating new meaning. In this sense it is an epilogue to ancient sacred life, where *everything* was meaningful. And thus art is perhaps a *prelude* to a new epoch of mankind, where the human being is *giving* meaning to existence.

LANGUAGE AND MUSIC

Phenomena of Nature — or not?

The human being feels uncomfortable having to face phenomena it cannot understand, describe or calculate. Regarding Nature, man tries to answer such questions through natural science. But it is especially irritating, when the not-understandable phenomenon concerns man's own being. Therefore one tends to treat specifically human characteristics and faculties like language, thinking, art or religion as "natural", i.e. proceeding from, or reducible to Nature. This is comfortable, because then everything is "natural," there is only "Nature." In this approach modern man considers Nature in the way of natural science.

But regarding specifically ***human*** sounds and tones it is easy to show that they don't exist in Nature: neither their elements nor their laws. In Nature, tones appear as sounds. But in the human sphere sounds are transformed: in speech, as consonants and vowels; in music, as relatively pure tones.

In all of the more than 5000 known languages, **sounds** are ***articulated*** tones. This means that they have a consistent *Gestalt*, independent of pitch or purity: a reproducible Gestalt like ***a, o, i*** or ***m, p, t***. In every language vowels and consonants form a specific and characteristic system. Our way of writing the letters can deceive us about the fact that a German ***"s"*** is not very similar to an Hungarian ***"sz"***; and it is equally deceiving if a language has only one letter for ***"n;"*** one should only compare the different ***"n"s*** in a word like ***"beginning."***

Today, through technical, acoustic analysis, we know very well the "how"[1] of the different sounds. But language-sounds do not exist in Nature. Sounds of animals are never the same as those of human beings; a cow never does ***"moob,"*** a dog never ***"wow-wow."*** This is also reflected by the fact that human imitations of animal sounds can be extremely different; for example, in Russian a dog does ***"gaf-gaf."*** Also, animals do not perceive exact sounds of language; even domestic animals "hear" vowels unclearly, and barely the

---

* From: Kühlewind, Georg. "Sprache und Musik." Unpublished essay 1988.Translation: Friedemann Schwarzkopf. 1988. Rev. 1991, 1992.

1 "form of the movement," e.g. computer-analysis (annotation by translator)

consonants. Those kinds of birds which can imitate human sounds are never able to produce them out of themselves.

The *musical* sound is *pure* **tone**, at least in the development of European music since the eleventh century — from the beginning of polyphony until the emergence of new tendencies in the twentieth century, like "concrete" music. *Pure tone* means that it consists ideally of *one* basic vibration and its corresponding over-tones (this is a simplified way of saying it, in the acoustic analysis it is much more complex). The easiest way to grasp the importance of pure tone is to look at the fact that, in the opera, one can simultaneously hear and understand two, three or even more texts when they are *sung* as duet or tiercet — if they are clearly articulated. In the theater, on the other hand, we already have chaos when only two texts are spoken at the same time because we don't normally use *pure* tones when we are speaking.

Originally, there was a ***speaking-singing***, speaking and singing not clearly distinguished, or not at all separate. Speaking-singing can still be found amongst archaic peoples, or in plays of folklore (like the Siebenbürgen Christmas-plays); a speaking on few distinct, almost pure tones (2-6) where the rhythm is structured after the speech, which happened in Europe until the time of Gregorian chant. As with the sounds of speech, the elements of music - pure tones - cannot be found in Nature either.

Neither can one find in Nature a model for other structures of language and music, such as phonological and grammatical rules, or musical structures of themes and melodies. Rhythms of speech and music are not imitations of natural rhythms, especially not among archaic peoples, who are close to Nature; their rhythms are too complicated. There is no "natural" or rational explanation why, in the Indo-Germanic languages, no word can begin with *"tl"* or *"mb"*, which is possible in American Indian and African languages. Grammatical, syntactical and musical structures (forms of songs, sonatas etc.) cannot be copied from Nature.

Such signs of ***abundance*** demonstrate even more the great ***redundancy*** (i.e. decreasing variety) in the evolution of phonology, grammar and syntax. It shows that they are not a "result," for example, of a need for communication. For instance, our experience with computer-translations shows how much easier the languages would be without many of these laws. Also, compared to their early forms, our modern languages are already polished and "used" — in every aspect simplified.

In cases where Nature is actually "imitated", already existing sounds and phonological rules of the respective languages are used. Otherwise identical phenomena of Nature would at least have similar names in different languages - which is not the case. Of course, from the point of view of biological usefulness (fight for survival, natural selection) all artistic and religious activities are "superfluous." This allows us to see them as characteristics of ***human*** existence: if a monkey or another animal would wear a necklace - out of its own impulse, of course - we would know that we are dealing with a human being. Any attempt to retrace and reduce human activities to phenomena of Nature or "natural" usefulness is unjustifiable with respect to language, art and ritual.

Feelings and Emotions

Music (if it is ***music*** for us) touches our feeling life. This is usually mixed. It contains subjective, uncognitive ***emotions*** relating solely to ourselves, and perhaps also something else, a kind of cognitive feeling, which does not relate merely to our egoity, but to the music. Emotions are "known," ***formed*** elements of the feeling-life: they are repeatable. ***Feelings*** — in the sense in which we use the word here — receive their ***specific*** quality from the perceived piece of music. "The familiar warmth" ("notus calor"), says Virgil about Aeneas when he is falling in love again. Emotions are analogous to familiar and ingrained thoughts. Feelings are more pliable, able to change, like ***sensing*** thinking, as it were.

The spectrum of emotions (such as well-being, discomfort, fury, envy, jealousy, ambition etc.) is quite narrow. When we hear music, certain sections of the emotional spectrum resonate. But this does not mean that music originally wanted to express, or play with ***these*** emotions. In essence one cannot really assign any of the familiar emotions to (good) music. Not even a ***Funeral March*** is unambiguously sad, it always contains some very light feelings as well. This becomes obvious when one reads how differently certain pieces or themes are interpreted by musicologists. The main theme of the first movement of Brahms' Second Symphony is experienced from "weightless suspension" to "longing for death". Concerning the feelings in music one could rather speak of a "coincidence of opposites", a joining of opposite qualities, where the polarities of everyday emotions (between serenity and sadness, for example) are experienced as ***one*** feeling color: The polarities are not mixed, nor do they extinguish one another, but on a higher plane a feeling appears, which dissociates after the experience into the polarity between "serenity" and "sadness" — on the everyday level of consciousness. A genuinely "unfamiliar warmth": a quality which needs to be discovered and recognized in feeling (in the same way as one finds ideas within thinking). However, if the experience is repeated, this feeling can be deepened and transformed. In every art that is experienced through sense-perception (hearing feeling or seeing feeling, etc.) we can speak about *feeling ideas*, or *ideas of feeling*. The unitary, undivided *primal sense* of the small child is *feeling* — before this sense is differentiated by the instruction of language and thought. Archaic people have also experienced the feeling which is emanating from Nature. This explains their technological and medicinal accomplishments, without having natural scientific analysis, calculations or trial and error procedures.

There is much linguistic evidence for similar coherence of "opposites". The contrary meaning of certain words is well known; for instance, in Latin, *altus* means both "high" and "deep." One can find the *primal sense* of feeling in French for example: *sentir* means feeling, smelling; likewise in Italian: *sentire* means feeling, smelling; in Urdu: *messuz* means feeling, hearing, seeing, smelling, touching, tasting; in Rumanian: *simtire* means feeling, touching, tasting, smelling; in Turkish: *duymak* means hearing, feeling, sensing, smelling, tasting, experiencing, coming to know something.

For the adult, the feeling of Nature is hidden behind words — words which are inadequately understood in a nominalistic habit — which is not *understanding*. Such words obstruct the awe and wonder for the phenomena of Nature. We know that this is still quite different for the small child. In the arts we are still receptive even as adults, but we don't have concepts for the feelings.

"Program-music" (like opera, for instance), creates the illusion that music tries to express our familiar human-earthly emotions. From program-notes, the "text," we know what kind of emotions we are dealing with. In pure music (symphonies, chamber music) such support is not provided. But we enjoy program-music (opera) even when we don't know the program-notes — if the music is good. In fact, without the text we would not so quickly be satisfied with our everyday emotions.

Logos-Structure

In Nature, one can find biologically superfluous phenomena in abundance; there they are *given*. But in the human sphere new ones are continuously produced; these can all be traced to the phenomenon of "speech" which, in essence, is not a natural phenomenon. Speech is not genetically inherited but develops only under the influence of a speaking environment.

It is part of human existence to transform Nature. This characterizes the path from the "garden" to the "city"[2]—both in its good and bad aspects. The transformation begins with language: phonological or grammatical systems cannot be traced to natural circumstances.

Through—and from—language the human being learns how to think. Thinking is surrounded by feeling (feeling of evidence) and willing (thinking will). In art, we no longer deal with thinking, but predominantly with feeling ideas. Today, this path leads from thinking to living thinking, from living thinking to cognitive feeling - the thinking of the heart - and then to cognizing willing.

Linguistics has always asked for the common characteristics of the several thousands of languages we know. Disregarding trivialities one can say the following:

1. Every human language has an appearing and a not-appearing part. One side appears outwardly to sense-perception, the other is a process of human consciousness.

2. The appearing part of languages has a discontinuous (in the hidden aspect) and a continuous structure: sounds, words, sentences, etc., on the one hand, ***understanding*** on the other.

3. The appearing part has a hierarchical structure; sounds, words and sentences etc. are integrated on the respective next higher level of reading understanding.

4. When we speak, the text is determined from above, from the highest level of the meaning (if it really "says" something). The meaning, which one wants to communicate and express, determines the sentences, words, and sounds — in this hierarchical sequence. In listening to a spoken text, on the other hand, one follows this path in the opposite direction.

Especially the process of learning to ***read*** illustrates the last two characteristics. First the forms of the letters are connected with the sounds. The next level (much higher) is the reading-uniting of sounds into words. Another steep incline leads to the integration of words into sentences. The ability to read means that the appearing part of language can be supplemented with understanding. This applies also to spoken text; the "reading-together" of its distinct elements *is* the understanding.

When we want to say something, we do not want to communicate a certain number of words or sounds, but only ***one*** thing, namely the meaning of the sentence, or sentences. But in order to communicate this meaning, we have to "enchant" it in the discontinuous form of a sentence. And the listener or reader has to perform a "disenchantment" to get the meaning from the sounds and words. This twofold movement — enchantment and disenchantment — allows the twofold possibility of being

[2] from the garden of paradise to the city of the new Jerusalem (annotation by translator).

free from one another, and at the same time the ability to communicate. Without the additional activity of the perceiver, the meaning cannot even arrive.

As long as the human being is not able to think abstractly, i.e. independent of language (nowadays, thinking already emancipates at an early stage from its instructor, language); concepts are supplied by the mother tongue. Through these concepts the outer and inner worlds — which would otherwise appear in undistinguished continuity — are structured into distinct entities. Concepts allow us to see where an object has its boundaries, what does and what doesn't belong to it, etc. Thus, in the first stage, the sense-perceptual and the inner world are structured by language. Then we search for connections between the isolated elements, in the same way in which we integrate a spoken or written text. But Nature is an exception: initially we are unable to integrate its phenomena with reading understanding: that would be the Goethe'an look.

Thus the human being stands in the world, practicing a "spagyric" art: distinguishing (*span*, σπαω) and uniting (*ageirein*, αγειρω). In doing so, man realizes his own being and the essence of the world, the meaning of existence.

The described structures of language and the world can be called *Logos-Structure*. Music also has this structure in all aspects: as tones, motives, themes, phrases, and larger, more encompassing forms. In the activity of listening, tones have to be united to themes, and themes to melodies, etc. This comprehensive listening is like the "reading-together" of a spoken text.

Self-referral of Meaning[3]

Sounds of speech don't mean anything other than themselves. The sound *"l"* is an *"l,"* an *"a"* is an *"a,"* in every language, independent of the written letter. If the signs have to fulfill a secondary function, as symbols for numbers, for instance, they must first exist as symbols for sounds. This is also the case with conjunctions, pronouns, prepositions and adverbs. *Because* means *because*, and *still* does not mean anything other than itself, etc. It is more difficult to grasp — and in the whole discipline of linguistics it is rarely noticed — that even·nouns and verbs are only pointing to their own meaning. If one means "table" one points to a variety or a class of objects. If one wants to characterize these objects, one quickly comes to a dead end: for even the lid of a piano, or the side of a barrel, or a cloth on the ground are able to function as a table. The word "table" points to the understanding. I know what a table is, and I can recognize its function in any form whatsoever. This means that the word "table" means its understanding, in the same way as "and" or "or". In other words, "table" also means only itself. What does "blue" mean? There is an infinity of shades, and beyond that, the most diverse ways to realize blue: different surfaces, transparent fluids, etc. I can designate all of these cases as "blue," provided I understand what "blue" means. In this way the world is created for every child through the words and their understanding. Language does not "designate" things, things which would be complete even without language. But—within the continuum of the *given*—language selects and highlights certain distinct units: things, qualities, gestures of consciousness (like "although"), etc. Every word creates a new piece of land within the

3 note by the translator: *"Self-meaning"* ("self-referral of meaning" ~ *Selbstbedeutung*) is the seeing of the understanding that *integrates*. For instance, a certain *blue* is "blue" only within a certain spectrum; next to a deeper (royal) blue it appears as "turquoise." The context into which a distinct entity is integrated is comparable to a language which consists of all its words. *That* is the "seeing feeling" of the Idea, of a language, a letter, a consonant, or a vowel, for example. The entire Zodiac is a hieroglyph that *means* the human being. The activity which sees it as a hieroglyph, that is the *being* and *essence* of the word-nature of the human being. It is the thinking that relates a concept to a context, which is *understanding*. This understanding is the seeing into the eye of the "ideality."

("Das Gespräch ist vieldeutig: das ist das Grundtrauma der Poststrukturalisten" ["Conversation is ambiguous; that is the basic problem for poststructuralism"] G.K.). If we consider our world of concepts to be a world where every concept is defined through another concept, we eliminate *understanding*. What we must notice even here, is the fact that there is someone who is able to "make sense" out of a certain configuration of conceptual-ideal systems. And the encompassing meaning of the sense of such a system is the guiding meaning for that which Kühlewind calls "Selbstbedeutung der Laute" (self-meaning of sounds). This "self-meaning" of sounds has meaning within the ideal-conceptual understanding into which these sounds are integrated: the same understanding out of which they were *meaningfully* idividualized in the first step. The Logos-principle is always guiding.

continuously flowing sea. If one tries to imagine a language which does not know a word for "but," one notices that it would be much poorer. One experiences the enrichment which follows from such a word.

In the same way as words and languages are creating new worlds with their structure of the continuum of the given Nature, in their producing and highlighting new gestures of consciousness (like "but", which cannot be found in Nature), so is music creating itself — like every art. As the sound *"a"* is demonstrating and *creating* only itself, likewise the Second Symphony of Beethoven *is* only itself: a new creation, a new phenomenon in the world of tones, in the world at large.

Language is not a *naming (be-nennen)* of things the human being could not perceive without names, but it is a *calling* into being *(nennen)*. It calls the things, and doing so they *become*, become distinct unities; they can be perceived and remembered, recognized and even be *re-named* - at a later stage. With this deed, the one-who-speaks-and-understands begins to identify himself as a separate entity within the entirety of the structure of the world: his path to self-consciousness.

Thus, language is also working within the *not-given* sphere. Conjunctions ("but", "otherwise", "without"), comparisons ("bigger") and adjectives ("small", "large") are sole expressions of our inner activity. One says: "a small elephant", in the same way as one says "a small worm" — these are two very unsimilar perceptions. With every word, language instructs the attention to focus selectively on "something" (the word's meaning and understanding), and grammar teaches us gestures of consciousness, ways and manners of understanding, providing systems of relationships in which the distinguished, separate unities are integrated.

By using *not-given* elements, *musical* tones, music also works in the *not-given* sphere. Music creates ideas of feeling which are brought to appearance in the audible sphere, in listening-feeling. Language uses the sounds of speech; they, too, are new creations. Every language presents different metamorphoses of what is *given* by Nature — like the tones in music. These two types of phenomena appear only in the human sphere.

Why are language and music requiring elements like sounds, words and tones, which only mean themselves and nothing else? Such a question arises from an inverted modern perspective: All *other* elements are only *coming into being* in the act of *calling (nennen)*, by way of language in the widest sense. A thing, seemingly *given*, like a matter-of-course, is the result of an individualizing structuring that "lifts" the "thing" out of its larger, whole complexity, because by means of a word the language has identified a specific understanding — the corresponding concept. Only later, after the human being has learned how to give structure (through the language!), is a "thing" the result of abstract thinking, independent of language, as are all scientific, technical concepts and entities. The *given* world is not complete without the conceptual structure, which is originally created by the language; this is how distinguishable elements and their connections come into being. It is easy to understand that real concepts, i.e. "understandings", are not the result of abstraction — i.e. the common denominator of the "important" characteristics of a certain groups of things — because a concept is already needed to select the things, and to find their "important" characteristics.

For *calling (nennen)*, language cannot not use already existing elements (this would become a "no-language") because they would have to be "seen" first, which requires that they have already become the things, phenomena and unities as a result of language. It is a consequence of our nominalistic orientation that language is experienced as a system of designations, a kind of "reduplication" of the "world". But without this *calling into being* we would only "perceive" (or rather: feel) an unstructured continuum. In *Truth and Science* Steiner calls it the "directly given." We have to learn the ability of structuring on the lowest level of consciousness, the reflected, brain-bound thinking, in order to apply the acquired faculty in a metamorphosed form on higher levels. To the degree that the human being is able to think independently of language (but still abstractly), it sees the things which are identified within the continuum, even without support of words. At this stage one would have to learn to expand and apply this faculty of structuring (now independent of language) to the next-higher level of living (imaginative) thinking and representing: as cognizing feeling (inspiration) regarding feeling ideas, as cognizing willing (intuition) regarding willing ideas and beings. By its very nature, music — or art in general — cannot be a reduplication, because it is a totally new creation, not a "translation"; it consists of new, feeling ideas. In this respect the human being is in the process of creating "new heaven and new earth."

The Effect of Language and Music on Man

An ordinary text does not change us, although its content may be exciting or even comforting, etc. An artistic text —or music—on the other hand has the additional effect that it raises the level of consciousness for a certain period of time: from the every-day level to a higher, lighter plane — if it is real art (classical music, for instance). And the consciousness sinks to a lower, duller, more "instinctive" level if it is occupied with a substitute for art, like entertaining literature or music. True art addresses the super-conscious sphere, the *source* of consciousness; substitute art speaks to the subconscious, our secondary instincts, which are not "natural." This distinction can help to identify whether something can be considered as art or not.

Logo-Structures, like texts and music, have the common characteristic that their sense-perceptible part needs to be supplemented by an inner process — our "integrating reading," as one could also call it. When we deal with a familiar or trivial text or a well-known piece of music, this supplementing happens almost automatically; it is hardly noticed. But with more demanding texts, or in attentive listening to music, especially in the first encounter, the supplementing inner act can be experienced. The words of a sentence are molten, as it were, and united in living, fluid understanding, into a meaning that was slumbering in the appearing part of the words. The enchanted sense, the embalmed meaning, is brought to resurrection. We redeem what was given in distinguishable, discontinuous appearance, and transform it into a fluid-living continuity, where it once originated. In music it is noticeable that we always experience it to be in movement. Yet, there is no physical movement: the tones and harmonies appear in a sequence, and remain the way they appeared, without further change. It is the music and our attention which are moving; they are not two, but one and the same intentional reality: the MUSIC; the same with a text.

The more the perceived is new for us, the stronger is the "activity" we use to supplement the text or the music; the activity is super-conscious. In the case of a demanding non-artistic text[4], one activates the super-conscious level of living (imaginative) thinking and representing. The artistic experience reaches higher because it works with feeling ideas. Our feeling is changed, and so are we. This is how art works: through the super-conscious supplementing activity which integrates the outer, perceptually given.

A reading that integrates and merges the single elements into *one* comprehensive understanding, re-enlivens and redeems the finished past form. At a time when mankind comes of age, the human being looks at its own past and dissolves it. One analyzes the forms as they have come into being (also in art), and uses them consciously, but filled with new content; and one reflects upon what has come into being super-consciously. Coming of age means to dissolve the compelling elements of the past; from now on one can no longer be satisfied with their effects. With this ability to look at the past, one assumes responsibility for oneself. Responsibility ("response-ability") is the faculty to respond: this is *my* answer, a new beginning, not a reaction, nor a causal effect, nor a reflex. The answer responds to the *call*, the call of the Word, the Logos. And therefore

[4]e.g. a philosophic text (annotation by translator).

the answer is always leading towards the common language of mankind, beyond the words of individual languages, to a *Michaelic language*.[5]

For human destiny, the consequence is the metaphor of the word, the metaphor of music. Words have meaning only within a whole language; only then are they *words*. Every single word contains and evokes the entirety of its language. Nevertheless, every word maintains its individuality, does not merge with the other words — which would be a dissolving of language. Likewise it is the aim of every single human being to become a word, a single statement or answer within the language of mankind, the language of the Logos, to become similar to the Primal Word, without renouncing individuality.

European, Western music has become polyphonic; every archaic music is monophonic. The road to polyphony can be seen as a development from the archaic union of the soul in a common folk or group consciousness towards individual self-consciousness. A true individuality acts socially from out of its inner freedom. Individuals, single voices, can reach a voluntary harmony. To make music in that manner means that I learn to respect the other voices, the other individual musicians, that I respect their freedom, so that musical togetherness can occur. But only with pure tones can one make polyphonic music; only then is a simultaneous sounding-together possible (like the miracle of an accord) where the single tones remain individual, do not merge into an average tone (as colors do), but produce an entirely new quality.

In music we are capable of such social practice, it helps us to reach a higher level of consciousness where we are united: as a model for life on earth. To be able to sound together even on earth, we have to learn to become pure tones ourselves.

[5]Steiner, Rudolf. *Rosicrucianism and Modern Initiation*. Lecture VI., Dornach, 13.Jan.1924. Trans. Mary Adams. in: *Christian Rosenkreuz (The Mission of Christian Rosenkreuz - Its Character and Purpose)*. Trans. Dorothy Osmond. London, England: Rudolf Steiner Publishing Company. 1950. p.172, 183ff. German: Steiner, Rudolf. *Mysterienstätten des Mittelalters - Rosenkreuzertum und modernes Einweihungsprinzip*. Dornach, Schweiz: Rudolf Steiner Verlag. 1991. GA 233a, S. 83, 93ff.

PERCEPTION EXERCISES*

In order to develop perceptual faculties,[1] one has to work with the perceiving attention; this means to be working at the same time on the relation between the every-day I and the true I. The autonomy for this work is found and originates in thinking; and on the first level one can safely consider the schooling of perception also an education of thinking; because what the perception reveals is determined by the quality of the conceptuality. If one can keep the thinking in a process, i.e. in continuous preparedness, able to avoid a falling into finished thought, one will immediately also have imaginative perception, because the thought conceptuality — ordinarily interwoven with the perceiving — would not change the living perceiving into a static dead past. If one has developed the capacity of living thinking, one also has access to living perceiving, because in both activities the I — the attention — has the same quality.

This is a long path, irrespective of the exercises of thought-concentration.[2] The first step is to re-establish normal — or rather, healthy — perceiving. Modern life trains a habit of informational perception, which is only interested in identifying the concept or labeling the percept.

Informational perception means that we establish what we see by a superficial glance, for instance, "a bouquet of red roses." We would probably be unable to picture the bouquet with our inner eye, since we have not really *seen* all its extremely complicated details.

This is why the first exercise is a straight-forward perception of a simple object. The first two exercises need no prior practice; the later ones require some experience in thinking.

---

* From: Kühlewind., Georg. ***Die Wiederbelebung der Sinne— Wege zum fühlenden Wahrnehmen.*** Chapter 8: "Wahrnehmungsübungen." Stuttgart, Germany: Verlag Freies Geistesleben. 1989. Translation: Friedemann Schwarzkopf. 1989.

[1] see also: R.Steiner, GA 322, evening of 2.XI.20;
G. Kühlewind, ***Schooling of Consciousness***, chapter "Pure Perceiving", "Perceiving as Therapy", "The Reading in the Book of Nature", "The Training of Perception", Rudolf Steiner College Publications, 4th ed. 1989; ***Das Licht des Wortes***, chapter "Das Wahrnehmen des Lebens", Verlag Freies Geistesleben, Stuttgart 1984.

[2] G. Kühlewind, ***From Normal to Healthy,*** Chapter 5, Lindisfarne Press, Great Barrington, Mass. 1988; ***Freiheit Erüben***, chapter "Die Schulung der Aufmerksamkeit", Verlag Freies Geistesleben, Stuttgart, Germany, 1988.

1. Simple perception

Subject: a pebble (not a crystal) or a small plant leaf. Time: 5 minutes maximum, half a minute in the beginning. A crystal is aesthetically not indifferent; it also creates some optical problems; at a later stage one can also work with crystals.

It is very difficult to give one's intense, and eventually undivided attention to an object that is not interesting. It is important that one is not burdened by worries (small or large), thoughts or feelings which accompany or go along within the intentionality, which could affect our attention; our defense would merely amplify the presence of what we would try to fend off. Therefore one could even make some kind of inventory of the most urgent and pressing concerns before one begins with the exercise, and say to oneself: for the next minutes I will dedicate myself entirely to the theme of this exercise.

One sits down for the few minutes of the exercise (the time is counted approximately from the time that one is able to be relatively quiet inwardly, not by the clock). ***One takes a simple stone or plant-leaf into one's hand, or places it before oneself, and observes it.*** If one has a tendency toward "staring" at the object, it is helpful not to put the object in the symmetry-axis between the eyes, but a little to the side. The distance to the object should be far enough to be able to behold it as a ***whole***. Details are of interest only if they are perceptible also from this distance. The requirements are simple, and in their simplicity they seem to be contradictory: if possible one should perceive ***in detail*** as well as the ***whole***, at the same time. The problem is, if one can behold the wholeness, it is difficult to see specific details, and vice versa. This contradiction shows the ambiguous nature of the pendulum swing: one looses sight of the wholeness, when one looks at details (form, color, pattern, surface-quality etc.); one also registers both consciously and unconsciously, if one is focused on details. It is entirely up to the individual, which gesture is easier to perform. We notice this difficulty in the second exercise, where we try to imagine the same object. Only rarely is one able to do justice to both gestures at the first attempt.

Therefore it is advisable to practice the two gestures of attention already in the first exercise. First one observes characteristic details, then, after a brief interval, one looks at the object as a whole. One should not move it closer to the eye if one wants to perceive the characteristics in greater detail; the theme is meant to be practiced in the given distance because a magnification-lens would reveal too many details.

One can try to register the characteristics which are identified within the structure of the whole by giving them a "label." With objects of nature one will soon realize that one is mostly dealing with unnameable details; we don't have words for what we see. When one observes man-made objects carefully, one will also find a lot of characteristics where this applies, like nuances of colors, the shine or reflection of light in a surface, the folds of a curtain, etc. In fact, the perceptual world cannot be described in words. Even the form of a quartz-crystal or tulip cannot be described adequately, so that another person could imagine it from the description without having seen it before.

For the start it is recommended to use only *one* and the same object for several weeks; this should be solid, like a mineral, not a living object. One can also extend the exercise by observing the object repeatedly, with brief intervals in between (1/2 minute), which are spent with closed eyes. During such pauses one can also insert a short concentration-exercise (in that case the pauses would be longer); thought-concentration and perceptual exercises enhance each other if they are alternated.

None of these exercises are designed to accomplish perfection: the aim is *exercising as such*. One can expect changes in one's perceiving only after regular practice for several weeks (at least once a day).

1.a) Comparative perception of man-made and natural objects

Now we do exercise 1. with two objects: a *man-made object* and an *object of nature*. The man-made object should be something simple, like a spoon, a match, or a nail etc. As in the first exercise one should observe the details and the whole with pauses in between. Afterwards one should register characteristic differences between the objects.

1.b)

After some practice in exercise 1., one should concentrate on ***unnameable, undescribable details*** of the object. Especially with objects of nature, one will realize how general and un-precise the designations are.

1.c)

One notices how the identification of unnameable, distinct entities is also changing the way they are registered: ***one no longer thinks in words, but notices, "registers" within the seeing***, without any thought in the back-ground. One can only say to oneself: "thus."

1.d)

In exercise 1.c) one can, in retrospect, recall soft and subtle feelings pertaining to the unnameable aspects, like: "there is nothing like it, it is unique." One should *feel the uniqueness.*

1.e)

During the exercise one should never be tight or tense. To avoid this, one may observe subtle differences in the color or pattern of the object, how it is lit, the effect of changeable light (sun or shade). If one isn't superficial, one will always find something new in the object. One always learns. One becomes familiar with the object, but never does it become boring.

The exercises should be done in a playful, easy, and relaxed manner. All knowledge, everything "known," also about the exercise, should be forgotten, of course not directly (that is not possible), but always by returning to the theme, exclusively, if possible.

When exercise 1. begins to show some results, perhaps after some weeks, one can try exercise 2.

2. Imagining

Representing — or mental imaging — means seeing, hearing, touching, etc. inwardly. For the sense of sight it means to create an inner image without outer seeing. This ability is different for everyone; normally it is not cultivated purely for itself, but mixed with thoughts and emotions; in the form of an exercise it is unfamiliar.

The exercise is to *imagine the object* we observed in the first exercise *with closed eyes, or turning our glance away.*

At the first stage, after a longer period of perception (1-3 minutes), one tries to create a mental image (1/4 to 1/2 minute).

Then one proceeds as follows: *perceiving* (15-30 seconds), then *imagining* (15-30 seconds), alternating 2-4 times.

The unfamiliar aspect of this exercise is that we would certainly recognize the perceived picture among other, similar objects (a handful of pebbles for instance). We could also remember the perceived if it emerged spontaneously as a memory-picture. But in every-day life we rarely have an alternation of perceiving and imagining. In this respect, schooling of consciousness is comparable to learning an art form, where one practices never used movements of the hands for instance, and becomes increasingly agile. Here one learns never used gestures of consciousness.

The representational image can be created in different ways.

The aim of the exercise is not that the object continues to "glow" before the inner sight after closing one's eyes, but that the object floats, as it were, as immediate after-image — even in complementary colors. This happens as long as the attentional will is weak: then one notices the physiological processes.

The inner image should be built up by the attention. At the beginning it can be "assembled" from observed details; this would be one's natural inclination. But soon one discovers that one can hardly build a strong image in this way. Then one can try to attain a global image by perceiving comprehensively. Both ways should be tried and exercised, also to benefit from the experience. Thinking works with details; but at first one can hardly differentiate or distinguish between thinking and imaginative representing. This can be learned by consciously exercising the two ways of imagining.

If one has difficulties to establish the *global image*, the following auxiliary steps can be recommended:

2.a)

One perceives the object (slightly from the side), closes the eyes, and continues looking at the object through closed eyes.

2.b)

One perceives the object, makes a brief pause, and then asks oneself (without looking up), »What did the object look like?« This means that one tries to activate ordinary memory which normally occurs spontaneously. The unusual aspect of the exercise is the intention. At first one doesn't know how to remember intentionally — *this* is the new gesture which this is to be learned.

It may help to try — in the imagination — to recognize and identify the object among many similar ones, for instance a quartz pebble in a bucket with similar pebbles. Or one imagines that the object is lost, that one is searching and finding it somewhere.

If one has difficulties with the exactness of the global image, one should be satisfied with the achieved level of recreation; with more practice the image becomes richer. The saturation of the image depends on the intensity of the *global* observation (which is not focused on detail). Therefore, if the representational image is weak, one should practice observing. We are used to perceiving quite superficially. After some practice, the representational image becomes quite intense.

If one cannot make any progress in imagining the image, even after longer practice of several weeks, one can try to proceed stepwise: to represent separately, first the perspective form of the object (projection of its spatial form into the plane), its outline; then the spatial form; then the overall color; then color-nuances in the surface; then the pattern, etc.

If the object has a perceptible weight, it is better to place it before oneself, to free the hand from pressure. Later, one can also try to evoke the image of touch, how the object felt to the sense of touch. The image of touch has the advantage that one cannot "think" it, which means that it has to be a pure imagination — if it succeeds.

Later one can use all of the middle senses, as well as the lower ones. With some practice one will notice that "undescribable" characteristics are by no means more difficult to imagine than those which can be "labeled" — which are rarely found in objects of nature.

When the imagining part of the exercise has reached a certain level of achievement, the exercises 1. and 2. are alternated: first perceiving (15-30 seconds), then imagining (15-30 seconds), repeated 3-4 times.

The imagining phase puts the ability of concentration — which has to be acquired through thought exercises — to a new test. As with all exercises, imagining also requires soberness; moods, fantasy, emotions, as well as already known facts about the object which are not discovered in the act of observation, should not interfere. The consciousness has to be content with what is actually given — here and now experienced — in the act of perceiving as well as in the imagining phase.

After a period of alternation between perceiving and imagining, one can experience that, at the beginning of the renewed perception, the object appears "differently", more radiant and fresh, "washed" as it were. At a later stage, intimations of new feelings can appear in the first moments. It is also useful to alternate the combined exercises 1. and 2. with a thought-concentration: The contrasting gestures of perceiving and thinking illumine and intensify each other mutually.

In this context one can try a little exercise: upon opening the eyes, one briefly looks at the object and closes the eyes again. If one can recreate the length of this "look" (which is entirely individual, normally around one second), one beholds the very first instant of seeing the object, when it radiates very intensely and luminously, because the thinking could not yet (or hardly) interfere in this brief interval. This is really a brief anticipation of the central exercise 3. (*"it lets itself be seen."*) One can also try to imagine the object after a brief glance.

The goal of exercises 1. and 2. is to separate the two phases of the pendulum swing, to cultivate dedicated surrender in perceiving, and being-with-oneself in imagining. In the perceiving phase one is already remaining for a period of time with one pendulum swing; gradually the phase of surrender becomes longer, which shows itself in a different quality of perception.

Comment:

Exercises 1. and 2. can be recommended for everyone, also for beginners. But one has to be aware that perceptual exercises have no distinct transition to meditation — as do thought-exercises; during the phase of surrender one is not on the level of mirrored consciousness. The thought-concentration, on the other hand, changes into meditative consciousness only when, in the second phase, the function or idea of the man-made object is becoming the theme of the meditation, as one reaches the experience of ***understanding***. But in perceiving, as one is leaving the level of mirrored consciousness, one is exposed to much higher ideas — ideas of nature, cosmic ideas, creational ideas.

Therefore the next exercises can be recommended only for students who have already reached a certain agility in the realm of thinking. In perceiving, the transition between concentration and meditation is fluid. This is why it can already happen in exercise 1., that one delves quite deeply into dedicated surrender (to a certain degree, surrender is part of every perception), which can cause anxiety, excitement or other psychological symptoms: the strength of the I is not prepared for the might and lightness of the encountered force of the idea. Regarding perception, one can say that we are always experiencing — passively "suffering" — intuitions, but, for our sake, in subdued strength. However, in ***intensive*** observation —perception — the attenuation is not as strong, and therefore the described symptoms can already occur in the first exercise — if the concentration is sufficiently strong.

Undesirable soul-states are usually foreshadowed by certain symptoms: the object becomes "larger," "comes closer," "moves," etc. At a later stage of the schooling all these experiences can be accepted as signs of normal development. But if they come along with fear or other unwanted psychological states, one should stop the exercise and for a while practice just thought-exercises for a little while, before returning to perception exercises — even if thought exercises ***seem*** to be more difficult (especially for those who experience such symptoms) than perception-exercises.

3. Central Exercise

If, in the course of these introductory exercises, the thinking, perceiving and imagining attention has reached a certain strength — for lack of comparison one can only say, when the exercises are proceeding without major distractions, and if one enjoys them — one can turn to the central exercise:

This is to try to make a distinction between the two phases of the pendulum swing of perceptual attention within perception itself — without a separate imagination-exercise. First I perceive the object with the gesture and feeling of "I am seeing it;" the attention streams, as it were, from me towards the object. After 1/4 to 1/2 a minute I briefly close my eyes (blinking), and then I open them with the feeling: "It lets itself be seen," "it gives itself," "it utters itself," in an entirely passive, receptive gesture; I make place for the object to shine at me. One remains in this gesture for 1-3 minutes, and then changes with a blinking back to the first gesture, "I am seeing it;" both phases are repeated once or twice.

If one does not experience a difference between these two steps of the exercise, one should continue to practice exercises 1. and 2. They are ***always*** the introduction to exercise 3. When one begins to experience a difference in perception at the transition to "it gives itself," one should continue to repeat the exercise in order to learn the respective consciousness-gestures better and better.

Exercise 3. was called "central," because the long road to perceptual meditation really begins with the second phase of dedicated surrender, when the thought-activity is at rest, which was practiced ***separately*** in exercises 1. and 2. One can create an infinite number of variations to this exercise. In the following some of them will be discussed as examples.

The first phase of the exercise — the conscious looking "from me towards the object" — also includes a phase of surrender, in fast oscillation of course; otherwise one would not see anything, but be immediately reflected by the object, and perform a sort of silent itemizing: as if, while listening to someone in conversation, we would simultaneously within ourselves judge, answer, agree or disagree with what we heard. Initially, one is also returning during the phase of surrender to being-with-oneself — more or less — but the pendulum swing is asymmetrically slowed down, so that the surrender is strongly prolonged at the expense of the other pole. This often leads to a temptation of wanting to remain solely at this pole, not wanting to perform the pendulum-swing back to being-with-oneself: it is understandably much "nicer" to let the object speak. Nevertheless it is important to return from time to time, for the following reasons:

a) If one does not return to the pure, attentive, undisturbed, waking day-consciousness, one will experience a tendency of wanting to "sleep into" the object, and a kind of "dusk" of consciousness will set in, accompanied by certain feelings of pleasure.

b) At the beginning, the exercise will only remain cognitive, if one also learns how to "come back," at least occasionally, also in order to keep the experience of surrender fresh and alive. The same problem arises in the meditation of a thought or a mental image: how long can one "remain" without getting tired? In those exercises, too, it is good to "return" from time to time. One can notice exactly when the remaining in the phase of surrender becomes a pleasant temptation, accompanied by a diminution of awakedness, and how long one is able to remain conscious in the exercise — with increasing lightness.

The first experiences in the phase of surrender are shattering or moving. They are described in different ways: The stone begins to breathe, to radiate; one notices — with a beating heart — that the stone *is*, and that this *being* is synonymous with its being-visible, its "speaking," its self-revealing. In other words: that *being* is a light being — cognizable. One has the experience of having really perceived for the first time — which, as a matter of fact, is truly the case. Genuine wonder, forgotten since childhood, reappears.

One can experience how the distance between oneself and the object is reduced to nothing, how one submerges into it — becoming it, how its boundaries dissolve. One realizes that *seeing* cannot be localized in space. The sounding or speaking of the object appears within feeling. Feelings emerge, entirely unknown, which are not self-feelings: they belong to the object, and are characteristic of it.

In this exercise one also understands the paradox, the more that one perceives — and is able to report about it — the more one is "forgetting" oneself into the perception; during surrender one increasingly experiences one's own identity — identity of the true I — with the object; when one is again being-with-oneself, the formulating day-conscious I can speak about the experience, because, during the state of surrender (or, in the thought exercise, in the intuitive understanding) it is identical with the true I.

It is characteristic of the experience of "it lets itself be seen," that it is accompanied by a feeling — as soon as one notices a difference to the "I am seeing it." In the course of the exercise, this feeling — not a self-feeling, nothing "private," but obviously a feeling of the object — becomes stronger and more differentiated: the progress consists in greater differentiation, which is the aim of the next exercises. It is comparable to musical education, where the hearing becomes increasingly differentiated — which the beginner cannot even imagine at first.

A further characteristic of the phase of surrender is that the object begins to become like a process, it "happens," it no longer simply "is." This can sometimes appear as a sort of movement, a certain "pulsation" for example; but the "process" which we mean is not a movement in space. One has the convincing sensation that ***being*** itself is a continuous activity, somewhat like a tone. Thus the object begins to "sound" inaudibly, which means nothing other than its existing.

Since the objects have form and color one can submit oneself in dedicated surrender also to those. This means to disregard the "rock" or "leaf," to look only at the color or form. One can pursue this possibility by immersing oneself into the ***color***, until it "lifts up" from the surface of the object, begins to "become" and to articulate itself; one submerges within it, becomes "blue" or "green," "tastes" or "smells" accordingly, i.e. one begins to feel within the color, feel like the color. One can also say that the color has a characteristic "sounding." In the same way one can delve into the ***form***, which can be brought to "take off," to separate from the object, in a similar way; and one can try to nestle oneself to the surfaces, to swim and move between them in a feeling savoring of the movement. One experiences the elemental being of sculpture. In the very same way one can delve into other aspects of the object, like ***patterns*** (the veins of a leaf) or figures in the surface, etc. These exercises of dedication to particular aspects of the object can be considered as legitimate preliminary exercises for the immersion into the object itself. The stone or the plant, even a leaf, is a wholeness that says something beyond its color, pattern or form. The ultimate goal is to raise this feeling to experience.

One has to be very careful when one tries to formulate the experience in words, because one can influence the experience as such if the description is not entirely objective; for instance, if it goes beyond the actual experience or if ***known*** elements are inserted. It is better not to formulate outwardly until one has developed the skill by way of the before mentioned wordless inner registering.

One can easily test the therapeutic effect of this comprehensive perceiving.[3] One returns refreshed and rejuvenated, as it were, into daily life. This comes about because, in perceiving, the human nature can unfold itself to a fuller extent than in informational perception. Fewer qualities of the object are lost, which otherwise constitute an accumulating burden for the life of the soul.[4]

---

[3]G.Kühlewind, ***Schooling of Consciousness,*** chapter 9: "Perceiving as Therapy," Rudolf Steiner College Publications, Fair Oaks, California, 1985. (Translation from: G.Kühlewind, ***Die Diener des Logos,*** chapter IV.: "Wahrnehmen als Therapie," Verlag Freies Geistesleben, Stuttgart, West Germany, 1981.).

[4]G.Kühlewind, ***The Life of the Soul between super-conscious and sub-conscious — Elements of a Spiritual Psychology***, chapter 2: "World-processes in the Human Soul," Lindisfarne Press, Great Barrington, Mass. 1990.

3.a)

When exercise 3. has led to a certain degree of routine, when a distinct and consistent difference is experienced between the two phases of the exercise, one can try the following modification:

- "I see it" — "it lets itself be seen";
- then (with closed eyes) one forms the representational image — and after imagining, again the gesture: "it lets itself be seen";
- representational image — "it lets itself be seen" within the image, etc.; i.e., after the first "it lets itself be seen," instead of repeating: "I see it," we alternate this phase with "imagining".

One can see the relevance of this modification in the fact that the imagining is no longer supported by the conceptual-pictorial memory, but by the feeling which emerged in the phase of surrender. Whether this feeling will remain constant in the imagining phase will depend on the intensity of the surrender, respectively the feeling in it.

Comment:

With exercise 3. one reaches the stage of perceptual meditation. There, one experiences that perception is no simple happening, rather a dramatic interaction between man and the perceptual world, a measuring of forces: To what extent can the human being bear the radiant "lightness" of the world?

The following exercises unfold according to one's personal style: the student should find his way by himself. The aim is to feel the perceptual world more and more differentiated. Three further steps will be outlined, merely as *examples*. But before these, another exercise, which can either follow or precede the central exercise 3. It requires efforts in imagining, but can lead to extraordinary experiences in perception.

4. The negative Image

One tries to see ***the negative form of the object***, or the space that it fills out. This is quite unusual, and therefore difficult, at first. Hence it is advisable to begin with a simple object, for instance a plant-leaf which is easier to see negatively, since it exists mainly in one plane. "What is the form of the air around the leaf?" — this is how one could formulate the task. Normally it is easier to imagine this hollow form, rather than to actually perceive it; this is how one can begin. When the exercise with a flat form is successful, one can move to a hollow spatial form. One can also begin by "seeing" the space between the branches of a tree — a conscious directing of the attention. That this is difficult, will be seen in the fact that one is over and again falling back into the "positive" object. It can help to imagine the air in color.

The experiences in this exercise are very individual, and they don't occur as often in the initial stage as in the preceding exercises. However, it can happen, that the characteristic quality of every surface lights up: in this exercise one experiences the working of forces, the activity "becomes" plastic, begins to "live" (even if the object is lifeless). This can reach a point where one experiences a kind of exchange at the surface, an interaction between the inner and the outer.

If it is a living object, a flower for instance, the negative spatial image can appear quite complicated and improbable (a dahlia for example). The flower itself will hardly arouse such a feeling of improbability, because we have become used to it, even though it is equally as improbable as its negative. This exercise leads to a fresher look, also for the objects themselves. Wonder, the primal gesture of all cognition, will permeate the consciousness.

5. Comparing two Objects.

The sequence of the attentional gesture is:

- observing — imagining, observing — imagining, observing — imagining, with the first object;
- then exercise 3. with the same object; i.e., "I see it" — "it lets itself be seen";
- thereafter, with the second object: "it lets itself be seen";
- and later: "it lets itself be seen," in alternation between the two objects;
- or in between: "I see it" with one of the two objects.

5.a)

Exercise 5. with two stones.

5.b)

Exercise 5. with a stone and a plant.

5.c)

Exercise 5. with two plant-themes.

In these exercises one can, as always, submerge oneself into the details of the object. But the comparison is always made between the *whole* stone, leaf or flower.

The comparison allows one to distinguish the feelings which are in the beginning more global. At first one can hardly articulate the differences. For the time being this is not so important; this is only attempted when the experiences take on distinct outlines as a result of the differentiation. "Outline," means to understand within *feeling* — certainly an unusual experience, compared to the fluid vagueness of every-day feeling.

6. Feeling of Qualities

Exercises 6. and 7. cultivate the differentiation of feeling. One can compare this process to the development of concepts in young children: the comprehensive, larger conceptualities are formed first, then their articulation into smaller and smaller details. First *color* as such (normally under the name of a specific color), then single colors.

Exercise 6. is to ask oneself silently (without thinking or verbalizing, but remaining within the feeling), *during* the phase of surrender (as described in exercise 3.), what the tone, taste or smell etc. of the object would be. The silent question is always related to *one* single sense-quality.

Gradually a sense-quality can be experienced in response to the question. The stone can have a "smell." It is probably superfluous to say that this is not felt by the nose, but inwardly, where also the ordinary experience of smell is having its source within feeling. The smells which are identified in this way are normally not experienced, and do not resemble any of the familiar smells.

If one looks at the "warmth" of an object, one can experience that one is not moving on the usual scale of temperature, but that the experienced "warmth" has other normally unnoticed specific characteristics, as if the warmth had color, for example. Similar experiences, but not the same, are known in art where one speaks about "soft," "warm," "hard," "cold" tones or colors, etc.

We have already mentioned that all sense-qualities originate in feeling. One can take an intermediary step to this pure feeling — which is still unreachable — by noticing its super-sensible metamorphoses: the feeling is not "refracted" by the sense-organs (like light by the prism), but by the living, feeling attention — a metamorphosis in which it falls like a shadow, as it were, at the surface of our habitual "feelings," as sense-qualities.

One can ask similar "questions" also about "shape" or "form".

7. Feeling of Reality

Before or during every exercise one should return to exercise 2., to separate the two phases of the pendulum swing of perceiving attention. Here one focuses the attention on the difference between perceiving and imagining. One asks oneself (in the characterized manner): "What requires more work on my part, perceiving the object, or imagining it?"

Through this question one becomes aware of something that is normally overlooked by the consciousness, namely that the effort which I activate in imagining is, in the case of perception, not produced by me, but .... ? One notices that the perception is always accompanied by a "conviction" on the feeling level, the feeling of reality, the conviction that the perceived *is,*[5] which of course is lacking in imagining. This feeling, not directly perceived and therefore metamorphosed to a more subconscious feeling, is the attribute of a radiance of ideas, which is the perceptual world in its true being. Since it exists in every sense-perception, we are used to it and do not even notice this feeling.

Exercise 7. consists in ***being attentive to this feeling of reality,*** either subsequently, or in a simultaneous feeling comparison of perceiving and imagining; the aim is to identify this sensation and make it strongly ***feelable.*** This comes about simply by directing the attention accordingly.

7.a)

Once the sensation of reality is clearly asserted, one takes two objects — two stones; a stone and a part of a plant; or two plants, or parts thereof — and compares the sensations of reality appearing within the perceiving of the objects ("it lets itself be seen"). By changing objects and circumstances (lighting, position) the feeling can become ever more differentiated.

7.b)

After some progress with 7. and 7.a one should consciously select two different kinds of mineral, for instance a quartz-crystal (or quartz-pebble) and calcite, and try to experience their quality in feeling. For the time being one should be content with oneself to experience without verbalizing.

[5]G.Kühlewind, *Schooling of Consciousness,* chapter 5: "The Reversal of the Will and the Encounter with the Logos-Force," Rudolf Steiner College Publications, Fair Oaks, California, 1985.

7.c)

Like 7.b, but with different plants, or their parts, leaves for example.

7.d)

One takes two plants (or parts of plants), but at different stages of development; e.g., bud and wilting blossom, young and old leaf, seed and sprouting or developed plant, and compares the sensations of reality.

8. Feeling of the Idea

Feeling — also the feeling experienced in non-sensual qualities like the "smell" or "taste" of an object — is the outer court of the ideality that is effective in nature, which nature "wills." This will does not originate in a being that is now creating; nature is completed, there is no actual interference with creation. Of course, this outer court is already a very luminous insight compared to every-day cognition. Yet it is not impossible to approach the will-like idea.

For this end one should direct one's attention to the *process,* which the object *is.* In the phase of surrender of the central exercise 3., it is one of the first experiences that the object is "happening." Initially the "happening" shows itself more and more distinctly as a feeling that radiates towards us; light, that can be felt. One "cultivates" this feeling of light, and notices its differentiation as it is received, in the way of exercises 5., 6. and 7. When the feeling of the object is sufficiently strong ***and*** differentiated, i.e. specific with regard to the theme, one can try ***to close the eyes and to "extinguish" the image.*** Again, this happens as an inner gesture within the exercise, spontaneously as it were, certainly not by thought intention: ***all attention is shifted to the feeling,*** provided that the feeling stays, once the perceiving is suspended. If this should not be the case, one continues to practice exercises 5., 6. and 7. The ideal would be that the feeling is not only staying, but increasing, because it is addressed with full attention. One immerses oneself into this feeling and follows its metamorphoses.

The next stage of the exercises is based on this experience.

9. The Will of the Theme

The phase of surrender of exercise 3. should again be directed at the "process;" one waits for the lighting-up of feeling, and then shifts the gesture of wonder, within the exercise, as it were, to the question: ›What kind of will is radiated by this feeling? What kind of will is "willing" in this process?‹ Once the experience of willing feeling is vivid, one closes the eyes and directs one's whole attention to the remaining feeling-willing. The next step is to try to extinguish the remaining feeling — within the exercise — in such a manner that one shifts the attention in expectation of finding something that is not yet "there," a presentiment, as it were. It is obvious that here one has to dispose of a receptive, objectless attention; this kind of attention must be reached entirely without interference of associations which could invade the space of the extinguished feeling. If the exercise is to be successful, one has to take hold of the "will of the theme" by means of the reversed will[6] — in a monistic consciousness, as in the experience of feeling — which allows the essence of the object to light up.

In this illumination of IT, the inner and outer become totally one. The experience already begins in the central exercise, when it turns into a process, and it continues in feeling. In these experiences duality is ***to a greater or lesser extent*** annihilated, compared to the every-day-consciousness; yet these stages are "umbriferi prefazii" (Dante, *Paradiso* 30:76), shadowy reflections of introductory prayers (before mass), however luminous or even blinding they may be.

In this act man is really adding to nature what she is waiting for: the creative willing idea of which she is a sign. From here the human being begins to understand the essence of nature as well as his own. This is the beginning of the eighth day of creation.

---

[6]G.Kühlewind, *Schooling of Consciousness,* chapter 5: "The Reversal of the Will and the Encounter with the Logos-Force," Rudolf Steiner College Publications, Fair Oaks, California, 1985.

FROM EPIPHANY TO EASTER

"A meaningless world is the only world that is meaningful for a being such as the human: for within a world already saturated with meaning, the human, with all its faculties of giving meaning, would be superfluous." (N. Hartmann)

A birth on the earth, whether it is an idea, a child, or anything new, is always a conjunction of something from above and from below, an inspired word meeting an expecting silence, a heavenly gift in an earthly chalice. The greatest of such births in the history of the earth is the incarnation of the Logos, which began at the baptism of Jesus in the Jordan. In this epiphany, the Logos - the Son of God - unites with a human being, the Son of Man. And this initiates the ascending branch of the history of mankind; this is a potential. However, the human being has hardly actualized it into reality. The "coming into the flesh" was a process of three years, culminating in the event of Easter.

The aim of this act of creation is to give the human being the capacity to continue creation, the predisposition for the eighth day of creation; having come of age, the human being could give new meaning and purpose to a world that has become meaningless. Therefore the source of creation, the Word, has to unite with man to "make its abode within man", so that the latter can become capable of beholding the radiance - the glory - of the Son. The Seeing of the Lord, from face to face, transforms him and enables him to perform the greatest assimilation - adaequatio - namely to rise to the rank of a "brother of Christ".[1] The first step to this stage is described in the prologue of the Gospel of St. John: From "children of God" to "sonhood", from "righteous ones" who do "what is right",[2] to those who "do the truth".[3]

This step marks the transition between the Baptist and the Lord. John the Baptist "came in the way of righteousness" (Matth. 21:32); the Baptist calls the Lord "stronger",

---

* From: Kühlewind, Georg. "Von Epiphania zu Ostern." in: ***Das Goetheanum — Wochenschrift für Anthroposophie***. #12. 24. März 1991. pp.105-108. Translation Friedemann Schwarzkopf.. Kühlewind, Georg. ***Journal for Anthroposophy***. "From Epiphany to Easter." No 56, Spring 1993, pp. 72-82.

[1]Chapter ***The Force of the Logos and the Force of the I***, "But Soon We are a Singing Song."

[2]1.John 2:29; 3:8; 3:10.

[3]John 3:21; 1.John 1:6.

"mightier" than himself (Matth. 3:11; Mark 1:7; Luke 3:16; John 1:15); and he, John the Baptist, has to "decrease", while the Logos-spirit must "increase" (John 3:30).

The Baptism

John the Baptist comes from an earlier generation, an age that is different from Christianity. The least in the kingdom of heaven is greater than he, the greatest among those who were born from a woman (Luke 7:28; Matth. 11:11). He knows this himself; this is why he speaks about the ***next baptism***, with fire and the Holy Spirit, which will follow his way of baptizing with water.

Through his kind of baptism the human configuration was to loosen enough — in the ideal case — to allow the connection between the consciousness principle and the organism to release, so that the consciousness principle could become more receptive for super-sensible truths. The one to be baptized had to remain under water as long as a life-threatening boundary was not reached.

Jesus also submits himself to this procedure, although initially the Baptist does not want to baptize one whom he considers superior to himself (Matth. 3:14), but then he gives in "for all righteousness to be fulfilled", or in order to preserve the continuity of the ever new teaching.

The report about the baptism is slightly different in each Gospel. Matthew and Mark mention that Jesus "went up straightway" — euthys — out of the water; Luke describes his praying; and in the John-Gospel the Baptist appears as a witness for everything that the first three evangelists described as an experience of the one who was to be baptized: the dove descending from heaven. Later, Jesus himself annunciates the opening of the heavens in his conversation with Nathanael (John 1:51), in obvious reference to the dream of Jacob and the heavenly ladder (Gen. 28:12).

The word "soon" or "straightway" can be understood as a key word. The fast emerging from the water, the praying, also the reluctance of the Baptist to perform the baptism, mean that here the baptism by water was in a certain sense a formal opportunity for the central event of the new age to take place: that the "Beginning," "the Firstborn" of creation (Col.1:15; Rev. 3:14) could unite Himself with a human organism which opened itself to him; now he could begin to permeate this organism. The human being was already prepared: this is indicated by the word "straightforward". In this case the submergence in water was rather a symbol. In the baptism with water the consciousness principle of the human being was touched for a moment by death, thereby ***experiencing*** the spiritual world. At the baptism of Jesus, on the other hand, it was the opposite: He was just for a moment under water, and the Holy Spirit descended from the open heavens in the form of a dove and *remained* upon Him, while John the Baptist is witnessing this (John 1:32-33).

One can understand the transition from John the Baptist — the culmination of the Old Testament — to Christianity as the change from baptism by water to the baptism by fire *and* the Holy Spirit (Matth. 3:11; Mark 1:8; Luke 3:16; John 1:33; Acts 1:5,2:3); in this context "and" means that *this* fire and the Holy Spirit are one. The transition points upwards: a sequence of metamorphoses of the *one* first principle: from water to air - spirit, pneuma - and to fire. One finds a parallel in Heraclitus: "Fire lives the death of earth and air lives the death of fire, water lives the death of air and earth the death of water" (Diels, Fragmente der Vorsokratiker 118). For Heraclitus the primal principle is the Logos - as in every demanding tradition; the fire is its synonymous imaginative image.[4]

The baptism with water lifted the spiritual part of the human being out of the earthly, mineral consciousness; the baptism with fire and the Holy Spirit is an entirely internal process which evokes within the human being the possibility to set the beginning for a spiritual path in the physical-mineral body, and to permeate this body with the achievements of such a path. In principle this path leads to infinite ***adaequation*** - assimilation - to the Lord (see chapter ***The Force of the Logos and the Force of the I***). The dimensions of this path can only be glimpsed: "Amen, Amen, I say unto you, He that believeth in Me, the works that I do shall he do also; and greater works than these shall he do; because I go on to the Father" (John 14:12).

The Opened Heaven[5]

The heavens are always open: it depends on man to see them. This is how St. Stephen's seeing of God is described in the Acts of the Apostles, the way he experiences it before his death: "But he being full of the Holy Spirit, looked up steadfastly into heaven, and saw the glory of God, and Jesus standing on the right hand of God. And he said, 'Behold I see the heavens opened and the Son of Man standing on the right hand of God'" (Acts 7:55,56).

[4]Kelber, W. *Die Logoslehre*, Stuttgart 1976; NT: Luke 12:49; 1.Cor. 3:13; 2 Thess. 1:8; Heb. 1:7; James 3:6; 1 Pet 1:7; 2 Pet 3:7; Rev. 1:14, 2:18, 19,12.

[5]see also G. Kühlewind, *Das Licht des Wortes* chapter: *Die Himmelsleiter*, Verlag Freies Geistesleben, Stuttgart 1984.

The experience of the opened heavens happens in the Old and New Testament always in a special and dramatic soul constitution: Jacob on his flight (Gen 28:12), the baptism as described in the first three gospels, the seeing of St. Stephen (above), the experience of St. Peter in Acts of the Apostles (Acts 10:11), and the passages in the Revelation of St. John (Rev. 4:1, 11:19, 19:11). The only exception is John 1:51 "Hereafter you shall see heaven open and the angels of God ascending and descending upon the Son of man." "Hereafter" can only refer to the consequences of the baptism in the Jordan, as a general potential of the human being in the future.

The opening of the heavens means in any case an opening of the human soul "upwards," to its super-conscious heaven, which is always present. Since the dove — the Holy Spirit — is "remaining" upon the baptized, he lives with his eyes continuously open to the heavens: this is not only confirmed by the miracles and signs which He does, but also by the immediate and direct knowledge of the future (Luke 22:10, John 18:4, Matth. 26:34, Mark 14:30, Luke 22:34, John 13:38), unuttered questions, as well as soul moods in his environment (Matth. 9:4; 12:25; Luke 6:8; 9:47; John 6:64; 2:25; 1:43,48,49; 16:30).

Due to the incarnation of the Logos in a physical body, the possibility for a way to immediate knowing has been given to contemporary mankind as a potential, in order to realize the ***receptive attention***. Because the Logos is present "in the flesh", within a self-experiencing consciousness, the consciousness is capable of directing its attention from within this consciousness towards its own sources. In other words, the consciousness can attain an autonomous self-consciousness on ***this*** side of the abyss that separates it from the super-consciousness, and therefore it is able to set the ***beginning*** from here: its own beginning. Through the incarnation in the flesh, the beginning — the primal principle — permeated the field that was subject to the Fall: ***this*** is the beginning for a ***possibility*** of redemption. And this ***possibility is*** the redemption. The self-consciousness cannot be redeemed ***from without***, without its own contribution. That would be an annihilation and abandoning of the free self-consciousness. But one cannot call the activity of the self-consciousness a self-redemption, for without the redemptive deed of the incarnation of the Logos and its further consequences this would not even be possible.

The formation of the abyss, i.e., the interruption of the continuity of the instreaming inspiration on its way to the level of the reflected every-day consciousness, could have brought the danger — and did to a certain extent — that the heavenly gift, in its unobserved phase of descending, gets distorted by forces adverse to the human being. This was counterbalanced through the incarnation: it allowed for the possibility that the reflected thinking could be a true image of the higher, living thinking, its undistorted shadow, the so-called *pura ratio*, a pure thinking, pure of all disturbing influences — if man wants it.

In order for this to occur, a spark of the Logos needs to be present on this side of the abyss, because the free autonomy of the consciousness has to be established first on the lowest level of the spirit if it is to rise from here to higher levels.

The Logos united Himself with the "flesh" even before the abyss had opened — or before it became too deep — thereby preventing a complete interruption of the connection to higher levels. The presence of a spark of the Logos in the mirrored consciousness made the *return* possible, the *turning* of one's glance from *appearance* to *essence*; for instance the exercise of directing one's attention from the perceptible outer form of a word to its inner meaning, or understanding. By illuminating its own everyday-consciousness, the human being can now behold a pure and strong experience of its own I.[6]

The Logos in the flesh: in this way the whole materiality is sanctified. The divine world enters into battle with the adversary, the Lord of this world, who helped to create the dead mineral. Therefore the great emphasis which the fourth evangelist is giving to the fact of the incarnation in the flesh.7

To a human being on the path, the opened heaven speaks through man's deep inner silence: through the receptive, momentarily empty consciousness. The I-being must become strong enough to "remain," even without having to lean against a finished — past — consciousness-element. This silence is described in the following manner:

> "What is outwardly spoken is the language for earthly life. What is coming to the human being from behind, as it were, reaching to the speech organs, what is not outwardly sounding as speech but approaching from behind and arrested at the larynx where it becomes mute and where the earthly language emerges instead: that is a spiritual language. This is something one might call the spiritual language which is spoken to us from the spiritual world."[8]
>
> "The human being makes itself[9] familiar with this world of inspiration by listening from out of the deep silence within the soul how the spirit, the universal Logos — but in its individualities — speaks to him; not in a physically audible speech, but a language which is not only inaudible, but less than audible, and just because of that, perceptible. And by finding the inner word that is not turning into the outer word, but is nevertheless inwardly activating the force which is

[6]R. Steiner, GA 17, chapter *Von dem Ichgefühl*.

[7]G. Kühlewind, *Becoming Aware of the Logos*, chapter 4, Lindisfarne Press, West Stockbridge, Mass. 1984.

[8]R. Steiner, GA 84, 15.IV.1923.

[9]We refer to the human being as "it," respectively, "itself," in order to clarify that we do not mean the male or female personality but the self-aware spirit that characterizes and expresses itself through the human being.

> otherwise revealing itself in the outer word through the mediation of the breath, the human being comes to know that world from which it has descended....."[10]

To create this "negative" silence one has to first place and hold a theme within the consciousness, with highest possible force of attention. The receptive, reverse attentional silence comes about by releasing this theme, by emptying the place of the theme within the consciousness.

The presence of the Logos in the every-day consciousness makes it possible that the human being is now able to enter the path *alone,* without the interactive help of a master, orienting oneself through advice and choosing among the given advice: from the very outset the master is already present within.

Death and Resurrection of the Body

In its structural composition man is similar to the word,[11] especially since his spiritual part represents a unique self-meaning; but also because this constellation has a certain twofold aspect: on the one hand a spiritual element, and on the other a form that is perceptible to the senses. In an analogy of the word, the pure relation between the two would be such that the appearing part would always be the adequate expression of the spiritual meaning; "expression," for other human beings who are communicating through perceptible signs. In the ideal case, the corporeality would be a pure, immovable mirror for the individual, in order to facilitate a becoming aware of the self-consciousness of the I.[12]

For three reasons the constitution of modern man differs from the ideal:

Originally, before the Fall, the human being consisted of pure spirit and a non-material, living, sensing spirit-body (living thought- and feeling-form), which was fully suited to serve the I for its expression. Through the Fall, these two parts which were *connected* before, are now mixed together, with the result that the consciousness-activities, which originate in the I, are releasing processes within the body. Due to the interference of the activities of consciousness with the organism, the mirror loses its steadiness and is distorted. Consequently, the very principle that caused the mirror to

---

[10] R. Steiner, GA 84, 21.IV.1923.

[11] G. Kühlewind, chapter *The Force of the Logos and the Force of the I,* "Man as Word."

[12] G. Kühlewind, *Die Wahrheit Tun,* chapter *Ostern,* Verlag Freies Geistesleben, Stuttgart 1982; *Easter* in *Journal for Anthroposophy,* No 46, Winter 1987, Hadley, Massachusetts.

move will be lacking: the processes which accompany the movements of consciousness are indeed not experienced consciously.

The further result of the Fall — the intermingling of the different parts of the organism and its super-sensible sheaths — was that the form of the spiritual body was not able to survive the interactions of the form-free I-being and had to break.[13] "Breaking" means that it fell out of life, which means a coming into being of lifeless substance. Life always proceeds in a formative process. Then lifeless substance integrates itself into the living form, and from that moment life is fighting within the material body against the lawfulness of the minerality, until death. Thus death comes about: now the mineralized mirror disintegrates.

The second difference from the ideal relationship between spirit and body comes about because the materialized body turns into a species of nature-being, subject to biological laws; inheritance for instance. With this, separate "natural" needs emerge, and characteristics which can no longer fully serve the expression of the I-being. The connection between the I and the organism with its line of inheritance is ideally chosen long before birth. In modern times this relationship is often disturbed by human interference ("birth-control"). All the greater is the task for the I-being to assimilate an organism to itself that is not ideally chosen.

In continuation of the Fall certain originally purely biological processes are employed for enjoyment, beyond the necessities of the biological organization (e.g., gourmanderie). Something similar happens to sensational processes: pure soul enjoyments or painful processes — emotions — come about, among which the negative ones are also giving a peculiar kind of satisfaction in their self-sensing character. The establishment of a sensation of selfhood — the egoity — is the third reason why the body is no pure expression of the I.

Self-consciousness arising out of the body is not cognitive. It does not allow one to know the body on which it deems itself dependent. But this knowledge of its dependency on the body also shows the spark of a consciousness which is independent of the body: otherwise this partial dependency could not even be noticed. This spark can be cultivated even within a body-related consciousness. A new self-consciousness can develop just by kindling itself in this *cognizing* spark, without having to lean upon the body. The spiritual self-consciousness — spirit-self — is now able to know and heal the

[13]G. Kühlewind, ibid.

body which is no longer used as a support for the consciousness, and can penetrate it more and more in a selfless manner.

The way in which the spirit-self is related to the sheaths of body and soul is a reminiscence from the world before the Fall, and is exemplified in the baptism at the Jordan:

> "It is necessary to know how, in humanity at large, the spirit-self is entering the consciousness-soul; it depends on the understanding of how the Christ-nature, as a particular cosmic spirit-self, came into the consciousness-soul nature of Jesus of Nazareth. There is no intermingling - according to Tertullianus - between the Christ, equivalent to the spirit-self, and the Jesus, equivalent to the consciousness-soul and all the other lower members; no mixing but merely a connection."[14]

Whatever is not speaking in the human being, is a seed of illness. The human spirit is a spark of the Logos, and therefore tuned into the Logos-nature of the world. The Fall and its consequences can be considered as attempts of forces which want to turn man away from being adequate to the Logos.

The Being who united itself at the baptism in the Jordan with the organism of the Son of man, has accompanied humanity also before, and avoided its aberration from the Logos-world through its sacrificial deeds.[15] Golgatha was its fourth sacrifice; the beginning of this sacrifice was Epiphany.

During the three years until Golgatha, the Logos entirely penetrated the human organism; thus He could accompany the human in death, too. The Logos became at home also in "this world" — an expression of John the Evangelist;[16] this is why the human being is now able to make a beginning also in *this* world, because it is the nature of the Logos to *be* in ***primal beginning***. It is the thinking that was potentially redeemed through the fourth sacrifice:

> "The purpose of the fourth Christ-event, the mystery of Golgatha, was to unite the thinking with the Christ-impulse, that the effect of the thinking as such upon the I would not come into disorder. And if we want our thinking to become more and more ordered, for our thoughts not to be in a mere chaos, but permeated with inner feeling and sensing, if a healthy thinking according to truth wants be developed, this is possible because thinking has received this impulse through the mystery of Golgatha, the fourth Christ-event..."[17]

After the Fall, death was given to mankind as a countermeasure against its degeneration. Through death, the identification with the mineral body is interrupted again and again. On earth, a similar independence of the spirit from the body is attained

[14]R. Steiner, GA 165, 16.I.1916.

[15]R. Steiner, GA 152, 5.III.1914; 7.III.1914; 1.VI.1914.

[16]G. Kühlewind, *Becoming Aware of the Logos*.

[17]R. Steiner, GA 152, 7.III.1914.

in every act of cognition, in homeopathic proportions: "With its cognizing part the human being is really always outside of the body and its life-functions."[18]

Man has learned to be a self — the self-meaning[19] — through the help of his body; his spiritual energy for being a self grows on the cognitive path. Through *cognition* he permeates the body and loosens it from the minerality, which is dropped as ash in the history of evolution. Because man no longer needs the mineral body for his becoming aware, the restoration of the pure, immaterial, living and sensing form of the body begins: it becomes transparent — a pure form. In the same way as the word is pure form, expressible in many different ways, likewise is the formed part of the human self-meaning freed from the mineral, thus becoming undecayable. This process was demonstrated almost 2000 years ago on Easter Monday: "It is sown a natural body; it is raised a spiritual body. There is a natural body, and there is a spiritual body" (1.Cor. 15:44). This is how it is in the world of the Logos: every natural body has its foundation in a spiritual body. The "deviation" through the materiality does not help to create either the self-meaning or the spiritual self. One can say that this process serves at the same time human love, which is — or would be — new in the cosmos. This love can only be learned within the materiality, because it overcomes this materiality already on the earth. Only a spiritual being is capable of love: the spiritual spark — if it grows. "As I have loved you" (John 13:34; 15:12); this is the new commandment of love: the way the bearer of the Logos has demonstrated this love in the earthly body.

Without an earthly body there is no economic life. And brotherliness can — could — unfold only in an economic life. The cognitive path leads to earthly love, to a solution of the social problems, and also to a redemption of nature. Through spiritual development the human being becomes the *sense*, the meaning of the word-being which is the essence of the human being; and at the same time also the sense of nature. Because for the human being, and in order to give him a possibility for its way, did nature follow man through the Fall, and is now waiting for its own redemption: "For the earnest expectation of the creature waiteth for the manifestation of the sons of God" (Romans 8:19).

---

[18] R. Steiner, GA 163, 30.VIII.1915.

[19] G. Kühlewind, chapter *Logosforce and force of the I, "Man as Word."*

WHITSUN

The Promise of the Spirit

Twice, the disciples of the Lord have the experience of being left behind by their master and twice they had been prepared in advance. The first time, they are left after the death on the Cross, having been prepared by the Lord (John, ch.14,15,16). The second time, the Resurrected One leaves them by His Ascension after preparing them with a few words. It is hard to say which of these two experiences is more painful for the disciples. Both times the coming of the Comforter, the Holy Spirit, is announced and promised to them. And in the context of this promise the disciples ask a question that is a result of their "not understanding." In both instances they do not understand the difference between a worldly Messiah, who "redeems" *this* world through His appearance within it, and the inner Messiah who, through His appearance, gives mankind the possibility to redeem the world through inner activity. For, how could a redemption come about, and what good would it be, if the consciousness of men would remain unchanged?

Before His death on the Cross, the Lord is asked by the disciple Judas, not the Iscariot: "Lord, how is it that thou wilt manifest thyself unto us, and not unto the world?" (John 14:22). Jesus answers and says to him:

> "If a man loves me, he will keep my words: and my Father will love him, and we will come unto him, and make our abode with him. He that loveth me not, keepeth not my sayings: and the word which ye hear is not mine, but the Father's who sent me. These things I have spoken unto you while I am still with you. But the Comforter, which is the Holy Ghost, whom the Father will send in my name, he shall teach you all things, and bring all things to your remembrance, whatsoever I have said unto you."

Parallel to this scene, as it were, a similar question and answer are reported in the Acts of the Apostles (1:4-9):

> "And, being assembled together with them, commanded them that they should not depart from Jerusalem, but wait for the promise of the Father, which saith he,

---

* From: Kühlewind, Georg. "Pfingsten," in *Das Goetheanum*. 66. Jahrgang, No. 24, den 7. Juni 1987, Dornach, Switzerland.

Translation: Friedemann Schwarzkopf, edited by Maria St. Goar and Linda Fleishman.

Kühlewind, Georg. *Journal for Anthroposophy*. "Whitsun." No. 49, Summer 1989, pp. 21-28.

> ye have heard of me. For John truly baptized with water; but ye shall be baptized with the Holy Ghost not many days hence. When they therefore were come together, they asked of him, saying, Lord, wilt thou at this time restore again the kingdom to Israel? And he said unto them, It is not for you to know the times or the seasons, which the Father hath put in his own power. But ye shall receive power, after that the Holy Ghost is come upon you: and ye shall be witnesses unto me both in Jerusalem, and all Judea, and in Samaria, and unto the uttermost part of the earth. And while he had spoken these things, while they beheld, he was taken up; and a cloud received him out of their sight."

Similarly the Ascension is described by Luke (24:51); here, the "not understanding" is mentioned only indirectly (24:45). The meaning of both conversations is probably this: only if human beings love the Word, when they are able to receive the Holy Spirit to be witnesses of the Logos, the Kingdom of Heaven can be realized on Earth: then the Messiah can reveal Himself and work within this world, through human beings, His witnesses.

Within the Cloud

The Ascension occurs after the last promise of the Spirit (Acts 1:9). The cloud by which the Lord is taken up, is not a natural one, as can be seen in other passages in the Bible; it is not a natural event. In the Old Testament (Exodus 13:21; 16:10; 19:16; Numbers 10:34; 14:14; Deut. 1:33; Psalms 105:39) the Jews are guided by a cloud at daylight; St.Paul refers to it (1.Cor. 10:1). According to the text, this cloud is Jehovah. In the scene of the Transfiguration (Matthew 17:5; Mark 9:7; Luke 9:34) Jesus is surrounded by a cloud — and the disciples too; Matthew calls it a luminous cloud. In the description of the Last Judgement (Matthew 24:30; 26:64; Mark 13:26; 14:62; Luke 21:27) the coming of the Lord is described in the clouds of heaven with power and great glory (doxa = radiance). In the scene of the Transfiguration, the voice of the Father is perceived in the same way as during the Baptism in the Jordan. In this sense one can see in the cloud a sign of the Father God's presence into which the Logos-Being is received in the same way. It proceeded from it. The chapters in the Gospel of John, describing the Parting of the Lord and the Prayer (John 17), speak of this "returning to the Father." It is not a mergence with the Father (John 1:1-2), but a state of oneness which is characteristic for the existence of hierarchical beings.[1]

The appearing and disappearing of the human gestalt of the Logos-Being in the more shapeless, unstructured cloud that is discernable in the background — while absorbing or

[1]R. Steiner, "The Ruling of Cosmic Intelligence present in Speech-Formation", trans. Dorothy Osmond = GA 183, Sept. 1, 1918; "The Being of Man in Relation to the Hierarchies" = GA 205, July 17, 1921; "Cosmic Forces in Man," London 1948 = GA 209, October 27, 1921.

giving birth to it — is the imaginative picture for the relation of the Father and the Son. After the Ascension, the concealment of the visible gestalt in the changing and dissolving clouds brings the "Wind of the Spirit," the fervor of Whitsun (Acts 2:1-4):

> "And when the day of Pentecost was fully come, they were all with one accord in one place. And suddenly there came a sound from heaven as of a rushing mighty wind, and it filled all the house where they were sitting. And there appeared unto them cloven tongues like as of fire, and they sat upon each of them. And they were all filled with the Holy Ghost, and began to speak with other tongues, as the Spirit gave them utterance."

After Ascension

Through the Ascension the disciples are separated for a second time from the *appearance* of the Logos-Being. The reports in the New Testament plainly speak of sadness and mourning (John 20:11; Mark 16:10); but aside from such feelings being normal, they are caused by the fact that none of the disciples comprehends the event on the Cross; they are not able to read the Scriptures — the Old Testament — with respect to the suffering of the Messiah (John 20:9; Luke 24:27,45; Mark 16:14).

Through the resurrection itself and the teachings of the Resurrected One, the disciples at least partly understand the true history of the Messiah. In the event of the second separation no text literally refers to sadness, there is even mention of a *great joy* (Luke 24:52); still, an understandable melancholy is discernable between the lines of Acts (Acts 1:10):

> "And while they looked steadfastly toward heaven as He went up, behold, two men stood by them in white apparel..."

We have to realize that in the experiences referred to here, joy and sadness are closely connected; indeed, they may be present simultaneously. This becomes evident from the talks of the leave-taking Jesus in the Gospel of John (John 15:11; 16:20,22,24; 17:13). The primal joy in the existence of the Logos-world, which can be observed when a child is learning to speak, can be present in all situations, no matter how sad from the human perspective.

The fruit of this soul-mood — characterized by abandonment and expectation — can be seen in the strengthening of the community, described as ***unanimous*** (Acts 1:14; 2:1). The Greek expression — ***homothymadon*** — appears again immediately before the description of the event at Pentecost, and also at the second "pouring of the Holy Spirit" (Acts 4:24, 32), where the following lines speak of the special spirit of community:

> "And the multitude of them that believed were of one heart and of one soul: neither said any of them that ought of the things which he possessed was his own; but they had all things common."

In the Spirit, individuals are not separated from one another, even if this Spirit is quite individually at work within each single human being: this is probably the meaning of the pentecostal event (Acts 2:3-4). The sphere that is common to human beings makes communication, cognition and world communion possible. The participation in the domain of the Spirit is at first *super-conscious*: this is why this soul-structure can be designated as *consciousness-soul*. When the human being attains wakeful consciousness on the level of *understanding* — the level of the living thinking process — the soul-configuration changes into that of *spirit-self*. *Homothymadon* is the preparation of the mind for the experience of the Spirit: of immediate, direct understanding.

Languages and Speech

Immediate understanding, without perceptible signs, is also present in every language that comes to appearance in the phenomenal world: as its hidden side. It supplements the resounding aspect of language, fashioning it into what alone can with justification be called a certain language. For what resounds or appears in writing is in itself neither "sign" nor "language" without the internal act of the one who is speaking or perceiving. It becomes "sign" and "language" only through the *understanding*, which must exist super-consciously in the speaker when he is supposed to formulate a sentence or, in the case of a conventional sentence, apply it appropriately. Likewise, the person who hears a sentence has to reconstruct its *comprehensive unity* — the *one meaning* — that is to be understood from a series of signs. This hidden activity is particularly evident when a new concept, a new idea, is being expressed naturally — by means of already existing "old" words, since new words would not facilitate understanding. Here the inner activity is without doubt accessible: how else could I express or understand a new thought by means of familiar words?

The *unity*, the meaning, the oneness — innate to every sentence as the content which the speaker wants to express, which is not the single words for themselves — is refracted in the different languages in various ways into words and signs and then differently reconstructed through the supplementing inner activity. This is why "*the same*" oneness, "*the same*" meaning, can adopt colors and nuances of feeling and willing peculiar to the specific languages; we can always experience this in the translation of demanding texts — poems, for example; hence the quotation-marks regarding "*the same.*"

Different languages can be distinguished by the extent to which the content comes to appearance or needs to be guessed through inner activity: which means to what extent the appearing part must be supplemented. In the archaic languages, the appearing part is relatively small. It is greater in *modern* languages, such as in Indo-Germanic languages. Regarding the hidden side, the reverse is true. You can imagine that the appearing aspect of language could diminish while the *guessing* inner activity would increase proportionately; thus the inner activity of understanding would become less structured and more continuous, as the part that is appearing in a discontinuous form is gradually decreasing. Ultimately imagine that *nothing* appears outwardly; then *everything* is left to the inner activity: this would be the immediate understanding. This has to precede the acquisition of speech in the evolution of mankind as well as in the individual human being, otherwise a language could never seize upon a folk-group nor could the child grasp its first words. This *mute* language could be considered as *primal speech: the* language. Individual languages always represent partial aspects of relationships, pieces of a larger reality, like single colors of a larger composition that unites all possibilities of colored existence within itself.

Human beings must acquire conceptual thinking and cognizing through the discontinuously structured word language. These days our thinking will soon emancipate itself from the language: we are given the potential of *abstract* thinking, independent of language. This abstract thinking — like a common denominator between different languages — is poorer in qualities than a natural language, in the same way that mathematical language gains its precision at the price of a wealth of qualities. But the human being could take the faculty of thinking independently of language and develop it further, namely in the direction of *primal speech*. This would require a schooling of consciousness. Thus a person could come closer to the effective, magical (unfragmented) primal language.

Healing and Pentecostal Speaking

In the New Testament we find two forms of a powerful speech: first, in the healings of the Logos-Being by means of the word; secondly, in the pentecostal event as a generally comprehensible speaking of the disciples, independent of language. Both kinds of speech are repeatedly used by the disciples in the different communities, in a more or less diminished form; they are described as the healings of the disciples and as "speaking in tongues."

The healings and expellings of demons are accomplished by the Logos-Being through the *undifferentiated power of speech*:[2]

> "Christ, of course, had to express Himself externally in the language of His day; the inner word which He felt within His soul, however, differed from the spoken word of ordinary speech; it was imbued with the power which ordinary words have lost, with the power that the universal language once possessed before it was split into separate languages. Unless we are able to form some conception of this power which is independent of these separate languages and which is found in those whose words are fully inspired, we cannot understand the power that dwelt in Christ, nor the significance of what is meant when we speak of Christ as the incarnated *"Word"* through which He worked and by which He performed His acts of healing and cast out evil spirits. It was inevitable that this "Word" had to be lost in accordance with human evolution after the Mystery of Golgotha. But, meanwhile, we have reached a stage of evolution which holds as yet not too much prospect that our efforts will be rewarded."

The inner speech that is normally the supplement of resounding speech was then practiced within the *entire* speech and this was the healing. The outwardly spoken word drew its power from it; the language in which it resounded was irrelevant.

Something similar occurred at Whitsun. What the apostles let resound outwardly was a *speaking in tongues*, a kind of "babbling" or "lalation," improvised combinations of sounds, no word-language with defined forms. Inwardly they supplemented the sounds with the *entire* language, and this enabled the listeners to understand them, as if they had all heard in their own language what was spoken (Acts 2:6):

> "And at this sound the multitude came together, and they were bewildered, because each one heard them speaking in his own language."

"Babbling" is the older form of speaking, even in the development of the child; it is closer to breathing than the formed word. It is the wind of the Spirit proceeding from the cloud and from the Son who has been received into this cloud. The entirely individual endowment with the Spirit, expressed in the image of "fiery tongues" (Acts 2:3), guarantees at the same time the community of all human beings and peoples — on the level above their respective languages.

In such phenomena the appearing side of language is obviously less important: the inner process is the essential element. If this inner activity is not "whole", i.e., not entirely equivalent to the undifferentiated power of speech, then others have to translate what is said (1.Cor. 14:13,18).

The Pentecostal event is the articulation of an aim for modern humanity. Through the mother-tongue we learn the conceptual structure of the world; then comes the

---

[2] R. Steiner, "Building Stones for an Understanding of the Mystery of Golgotha" = GA 175, April 10,1917.

development of the faculty to give structure, without resounding or imagined word-language. Actualizing this potential, not on the abstract level below the language but in the living sphere above language, is the practice of spiritual scientific meditation. The non-appearing *speech* opens unmanifest worlds: worlds unreachable through sense-perception. The first of these worlds is that of ***living knowing***, the sphere of life, the world of Imagination.

In as much as the contents of speaking are drawn from these otherwise closed worlds, the language used for expression can regain its almost lost life: for it originated in these worlds. The *essence* of the human word does not belong to the world of sense perception.

FROM WHITSUN TO MICHAELMAS

1. Decrescendo of the Given

If one considers the history of consciousness of mankind under the aspect of what is *given* and what is not given, one sees three major epochs with continuous transitions.

In the first epoch the whole life of consciousness is *given*. The human being lives in a consciousness that is the last manifestation — an offshoot as it were — the last wave of higher beings: no independent thinking, no I-consciousness. Language is still a cultic ritual in the form of speaking/singing; it is not used in everyday life: there the soundless communication of the group soul predominates, or in other words, the collective consciousness. The necessary knowledge is given without having to ask for it; perception is not yet separated from thinking.

The separation of perception and thinking characterizes the second epoch. With it the perceptual world — which is still given — needs to be explained and the explanations are found in the thinking which is mostly given as well; but through the pedagogy of the languages a kind of thinking develops gradually that no longer relates to the perceptual world. At the end of this epoch questions arise as signs that at this stage not everything is given any longer — neither are the questions. It takes a long time until the ability of questioning becomes a general human faculty. The communion with higher intelligences becomes weaker and weaker to the extent that the life of consciousness is more and more in touch with the bodily apparatus. An abyss which becomes continuously deeper and wider causes the separation and independence of the human consciousness from above. With the formation of this abyss, the egoity of the human being, which was initially absent, begins to develop under the influence of adversary forces which were for a certain extent necessary for human development and therefore admitted. "Inspirations" are now entering from two directions: from the superconscious above which reaches into the world and consciousness of higher beings; and the subconscious below from where the adversary forces are whispering, forming the egoity.

---

* from: Kühlewind, Georg. "Von Pfingsten zu Michaeli." in: *Das Goetheanum — Wochenschrift für Anthroposophie*. Dornach, Switzerland. Nr. 22, 30. Mai 1993, pp. 225-227.

If this were the complete situation which modern man had to face, it would seem hopeless, especially regarding human freedom. But this freedom can come about through the predisposition for the creative ability of beginning through the incarnation of the Logos, through its embodiment into the weak human soul which is affected by the egoity. The fact that a spark of the Logos which was in the primal beginning, is present, gives the human being a faculty to reflect consciously upon itself, upon its own consciousness, at every moment. If this conscious reflection, the gesture of the consciousness-soul, which cannot be given, is intensive enough the true I awakens within the soul. If this awakening is cultivated and repeated from time to time, the ego, the selfhood approaches the true I, individualizes the superconsciousness and makes it consciousness, and can ultimately unite with the true I. We live at the end of this second epoch.

The third epoch — in the future — would be the day of creation of the human being (the expression is to be understood in every possible meaning) whose beginnings can be found in art, pedagogy, in bio-dynamic agriculture, etc. In this epoch of consciousness the human being is given even less without its own contribution. Without human effort, without active attention, even perception will render less and less.

The original Pentecost happens already under the sign of this general decrescendo of the given. The Lord has to disappear from the sphere of visibility, so that the internalizing and activation of the embodied logos spark can happen. The unanimous prayer of the Apostles allows for the entering of the Holy Spirit and its revelation.

> "But I tell you the truth. It helps you that I leave. Because if I don't leave, the Comforter Spirit could not come to you; but when I pass on, I will send it to you" [John 16:7].

Now a transitional period follows where nothing is given any longer ***completely***. The given is the perception which remains for the human being as a gift of grace, but it has to be interpreted and ***completed*** through the actively acquired thinking, or should be completed so that ***reality*** can come about; this can no longer be given. No text, no mantra, no meditation can be given completely, neither as text nor as image, without the understanding activity of the perceiver (originally the text used to bear the force of understanding within itself). Every given is ***sign***, whose sense has to be found or should be found individually — this is the fundamental trauma of post-structuralism. The world of signs becomes a provocation calling for its interpretation by the human being, waiting for the solution of the riddle which it is, its redemption.

2. The Primal Word

The acoustical or optical appearance of the human word always has to be completed by hidden processes of consciousness so that it can be *wording*. Today the complimenting activity for the spoken is the thinking, for phenomena of art it is the cognizing feeling, for the cultic-ritual language of gestures it is the knowing receptive ("reversed"[1]) will. United, the two aspects constitute the reality of the human word; the sense perceptual aspect for itself, which appears with the separation of the word from its source, is not wording. It is like a seed which germinates in the fertile soil of a consciousness.

The human languages — creations of super-human intelligences — are partial manifestations of the archetypal language through which the creation, and later the healings and miracles of the Lord have happened.[2] This archetypal language had no sense-perceptually appearing outer side, therefore it was the *whole* language. The human languages are very different with respect to the relation of their appearing and hidden parts: the predominantly analytical languages (e.g., French) manifest more sense-perceptual elements and therefore require less completion by the consciousness; the archaic languages (e.g., American Indian languages) are "sparse," kindling much more of the guessing intuition. At the age of the consciousness soul the internalizing of grammar begins its simplification; the evolution turns around in the direction of less manifestation — less is given.

At the same time, thinking emancipates from language, first in the abstract direction.[3] Scientific-technical concepts are not given by the languages (e.g., gravitational point), and the corresponding forms of thinking are only given rudimentarily by the Indo-European languages. But a modern aim would be the body-free and wordless meditation from where the languages can again be enlivened when the spiritual investigator puts his experiences into words.[4]

The creation of nature happened through the "mute" language. Since Anthroposophy strives to really understand nature as text, every analytical, every outer description is unsuitable, since we are not analyzing in reading either; we don't draw conclusions from the form of the letters; reading consists in the completion of the signs to meaning. Nature

---

1 Steiner, R., GA 20, Chapter Ausblicke.

2 Steiner, R.., GA 175, 10th and 12th of April, 1917; GA 307, 17 Aug. 1923 (evenings).

3 Steiner, R., GA 83, 3 Jun 1922; GA 197, 21 Sep 1920; GA 199, 11 Sep 1920.

4 Steiner, R., GA 271, 5 and 6 May 1918.

also *speaks* a *mute* language unapproachable by measuring, weighing and calculating. It cannot be understood by dialectic thinking.

The ancient man was able to perceive the mute language of Nature through his soul life and this enabled him to deal with Nature without analytical science to produce great technical and other achievements — buildings, ceramics, metallurgy, medicine, agriculture, etc.

3. Increasing Silence

In ancient times the Idea, the understanding of the perceived, was also ***given*** together with and through perception. Therefore, the reality was received in its ***truth***. Together with the perception of the text by a priest, sage, ruler, "from God's grace", the power of understanding was given simultaneously. All of this became increasingly silent until it turned entirely mute. Especially in the *reading* of the texts, the human being turned deaf and blind; but also the source has withdrawn from the given texts. Sensitive people feel that something is missing. Pascal looked at the starry heavens and had to say: "Cette silence éternelle m'effraie" (This eternal silence gives me fear.).

There are no more appearances of divinities, rather the conviction grows that God is dead. This is connected with the fact that sense-perception becomes the guarantor of reality. The fact that what we call sense-perceptual is permeated with our conceptualities is forgotten and for sense-perception only the finished ready-made is accessible. What is now flowing from pen to paper is sense-perceptible, but it is not that which is still living in the process of creation, neither is it the one who creates. Ancient people were able to pray to the images of divinities because they had always conceived the sense-perceptual as a sign that is to be completed by inner work, and they were able to perform this work because their "thinking" (which *we today* are calling thinking) was still livingly inspired. When this life is lost, divine images turn into mute idols. The only experience which remains for modern man is sense-perception through which the mighty ideas of nature are still working, evoking in the human being the momentary presence. Therefore, sense-perception is still accompanied by a feeling-of-reality, but not the thinking or representing.

The impossibility to behold the essence of the divine through the more or less frozen thinking that is supported by the brain became conscious in the so-called Negative Theology. It appears in the sixth century in the writings of Dionysius Areopagita and is continued in the work of Scotus Eregina, later through Bernard Von Clairveaux and for the last time by Nicholas Cusanus. The Negative Theology is founded on the cognizing feeling as experienced with regard to religious truths, to faith, whose fruits the thinking is no longer able to express and mediate because it has already separated itself from this feeling. In spite of its justification and inner truth, this theology works counter to the great aim of scholasticism: to unite faith and cognition. And ultimately this type of theology contributes to a final separation of these spheres and even later to a drying up of faith. Because of the collapse of scholasticism, cognition lost its sources and entirely addresses sense perception, forgets the conceptualizing activity in perception, forgets its interpretation through thinking and generally forgets the process of thinking as such, the source of thoughts (because it is no longer experienced but merely a temporarily brief flashing, a "finding") and clings to sense-perception which is *nowadays given* as reality — and thus less and less is given. The false theory will become reality if the human being will not do anything against it: the brain will think, not the human being, and the senses will be *stimulated* instead of the human being perceiving through the senses. The potential attention is more and more occupied by the self feeling, the egoity, and is less and less extended through the senses in order to perceive; finally, it is really merely the senses which are stimulated. This is the way towards autism, towards complete "experiencelessness." The outer and the inner worlds become mute.

The mute worlds are filled with meaninglessness, with deeds, things and human activities which are not speaking, not sharing, not communicating. That is the noise which takes the place of language of the spirit; it is difficult to bring to a rest. Yet this noise cannot cover the deep silence even though it came about as a substitute because of the lacking of divine speaking. An aspect of this noise is also the seeking for bodily, not-speaking sensations which took the place of spiritual experiences.

Humanity faces an epoch where, in practice, nothing is given any more. First the inner voice turns silent, and one can already feel how less and less is given through sense-perception: most of the time we perceive merely *informatively*, i.e., until we can determine *what* the perceived is, without having seen it really, in a manner that it could be pictured in its reality.

If the Orphean tradition speaks about the silence at the beginning of the world (before the sounding of the creative word), the world is now again enveloped in silence. She is waiting for the word of man.

At this stage, that which is called "experience" has to be acquired actively by the human being; everything else coming to man without effort, even the expectation of such gifts, is an old, antique gesture. In that sense even the experience of God is no longer given — the human being would have to chisel, see and hear its divinity from out of this absence, missing and lacking. In this process he finds help in the principal of the kind of absence which is *the strongest presence*: the absence of *something* or *someone*. This kind of absence is the provocation or stimulation of the creative ability of the human being. The lacking sense of existence, the lacking voice of the divinity calls forth and activates the faculty of giving meaning, the human being's faculty of the Word.

Creation is the only place of human freedom; it consists not in choosing between *given* possibilities (e.g., between two options), but in producing a not-given possibility. In the activity of creating, the everyday I and the true I coincide, as it happens also in every surrender to the sources: of perception, or the inner source where the new originates, new ideas, works of art, or simple human gestures of intensified attention, as for instance the act of forgiving.

The step into freedom, to create an activity, conceals a paradox: no unfree step can lead to freedom, no unfree way — one could also say *no way* which is already-given. Freedom or intuition is an event of grace, without "why," uncalculable because it is above rationality. However, this jump can be prepared, its obstacles can be removed. Its happening is made possible just because of the eternal presence — from the beginning — of the true I that inhabits the super-conscious part of the human soul, reaching into the spiritual sphere, the consciousness of higher being. The act of creation comes about through the union (during the time of creating) of the true I with the everyday I, which forgets itself into the true I, sleeping into the true I and executing its impulses in the everyday world. Thus every moment is potentially free, if the possibility of freedom is seized. When intuition enters the human being, freedom becomes actuality effective activity, here and now in spirit mindfulness.

Thus the celebration of Michaelmas, just because it has no tradition, calls us to learn to live in the pure wordless element of meanings, in a continuous seizing of free moments which are always there and which are waiting for this being seized. This means to *actualize* — in the activity of manifesting in the world of experience — the free step towards the divinity which is remaining absent and waiting.

> Awareness is not hidden. But you can find it right now. It is only now.[5]

[5] Bodhidharma, *The Zen Teaching of Bodhidharma,* translated by Red Pine; San Francisco, California: North Point Press, 1989; p. 35.

CHRIST AND MICHAEL

The Ideas of Nature

Nature speaks a silent language, this is how it was created, namely through the *complete* language: its various aspects and fragments appear in the spoken human languages. Nature is a sign and an expression of mighty ideas, which are willing and feeling Divine beings. At our first encounter we can barely endure them. Once in a while, through *feeling sensory attention* we can touch their outer bounds. The power from whence these ideas are streaming to the human being, is Michael.[1] Therefore, His spiritual image is so important for humanity, especially at a time when our relationship to Nature has to be newly established — if we don't want to destroy her entirely. To understand the meaning of Michael's mission means to establish — parallel to the natural scientific way of thought — a "reading," understanding the relationship to the truth of natural objects:

> Today one has to cultivate the faculty to speak about Nature according to the developmental stage of the consciousness-soul. One has to understand the purely natural scientific way of thought. But one should also learn to speak *about Nature* — that means *feel* — in a manner that is adequate to the Christ. We are supposed to learn the Christ-language not only in a sense of redemption from Nature, not only via the soul and the Divine, but through the cosmos.[2]

The Michael-revelation gives love to the heart, so that the human being can live in the Divine creation in accordance with the spirit.[3] This means that the human being practices love in relation to the outer world.[4] This love for the outer world can prevent us from

---

* from: Kühlewind, Georg. "Christus und Michael." in: *Das Goetheanum — Wochenschrift für Anthroposophie*. Dornach, Switzerland: Allgemeine Anthroposophische Gesellschaft, 27 September 1992, No. 39.

1 Steiner, R. GA 26, 17.VIII.1924.

2 Steiner, R. GA 26, 2.XI.1924.

3 Steiner, R. GA 26, 9.XI.1924; 23.XI.1924.

4 Steiner, R. GA 26, 23 XI 1924.

unmeasured self-love; this is why perceptual exercises practiced with increased intention — and if possible in feeling — have such a great therapeutic effect.[5]

At the time of scholasticism it was a basic conviction that ideas live within things, or at least that the things are the coagulated traces of things. This view goes back to much earlier times. It was summarized in the sentence: omne ens verum — All being is true. "True," in this context means the Logos-quality, as we still find it in the German words of "ge*wahr*werden" (becoming aware of the ***truth*** of something) and "*wahr*nehmen" (beholding the ***truth***), which means to be able to grasp that which is unconcealed, transparent and knowable. The things of Nature are *cognized* by God; this is how they were created; for the human being they are knowable in principle, i.e., as a possibility, because they are made of the light of the Word in which the human being can participate:[6] "the reality of things is their light,"[7] as it were. Here "actualitas" is translated as *reality*, in the sense of effectivity, self-realization. Behind this we find two implicit convictions silently covibrating, difficult to retrace by the modern human being. The first is: not only do things *exist*, but they are ***happening*** (actualitas), like a fountain, or like wind (the Greek word for wind is "pneuma" — πνευμα — which also means "spirit"). Secondly, this ***happening*** occurs in God's seeing of the things.[8] This seeing, the seeing of God and the seeing of the human being, is a beholding of essence; a seeing of the universals in things; these universals — instilled by God's seeing into the things — "are their light," as it were, their suchness or being-*that*, which appears to the human being.

The view that Nature is a Logos creation — and therefore knowable in its essence, *readable*, text-like — was already lost at the end of scholasticism (William Ockham); later it reappears only sporadically through a few individual spirits like Paracelsus, Böhme, Baader, Novalis, Goethe. The attitude of natural science — analytically oriented to causality — excludes a text-like, readable perspective of Nature: a text comes about not through causality (the words or sounds are not causing one another) and cannot be integrated and read by way of analysis.

---

5 Kühlewind, G. *Schooling of Consciousness*. Chapter entitled "Perceiving as Therapy." Fair Oaks, California: Rudolf Steiner College Publications 1986. Also in: *Die Diener des Logos*, Chapter "Wahrnehmen als Therapie." Stuttgart, Germany: Verlag Freies Geistesleben, 1981.

6 Pieper, J. *Wirklichkeit der Dinge*: Munich, Germany: Kösel Verlag. 1966.

7 "Ipsa actualitas rei est quodam lumen ipsius." Thomas Aquinas, *De causis* 1:6.

8 Augustinus *Confessiones*. 13:38; compare also *de Trinitate*, 6:10.

Wording Above the Word

Because Michael is the spiritual force which mediates the ideas of the things of Nature to humanity — not the *names,* but the ideas, transcending the human level — the way to Michael also means an elevation of consciousness to wordless thinking, the sphere where human thoughts originate, where they are not yet embedded in the "veil" of words.[9] This is also the secret and the key for meditative sentences. One has to sustain the sentence — the meaning to which all words of a sentence are pointing — in consciousness, without words, so that the living meaning[10] elevates the human spirit until the higher meaning of the sentence appears. The actuality of wordless "thinking" is frequently emphasized by Steiner,[11] especially in connection with the impulse of Michael. At one occasion the ***understanding-above-languages*** is even described as the sense of Anthroposophy:

> If we want to conceive Anthroposophy in the right sense — from an historical point of view for the present historical moment — it would mean to find an international means of communication across the entire world, through which one human being finds the other human being, a means of communication which lies one level higher than language. . . The way to the spirit of the human being we have to find above language. . . That means. . . to seek for a language of thoughts, as it were.
>
> The ordinary language of sounds moves in the air, lives still in the sense-perceptual sphere. The language Anthroposophy is striving for will move in the pure element of light — this is meant in more than a merely metaphorical sense — that passes from soul to soul from heart to heart.[12]

Body-free thinking is above language; languages need *signs,* and, since they are sense-perceptual, the signs are brought forth and perceived by the body.

The wordless language of thinking — living thinking — leads the human being into a spiritual sphere where Michael abides in our age:

> The age which is now dawning requires that humanity considers a world which is experienced spiritually, directly bordering the physically experienced world, and where one can find that which was here characterized as Michael-being and Michael-mission.[13]

The sense of this mission is that through this mission humanity again finds a "reading," i.e., understanding the relationship to Nature, the text of the cosmos. In this way the

---

[9] Kühlewind, G. *Die Diener des Logos*, Chapter entitled "Das wortlose Denken," Stuttgart, Germany: Verlag Freies Geistesleben, 1984.

[10] Steiner, R. GA 114, 21.IX.1909.

[11] Steiner, R. GA 83, 3.VI.1922; GA 137, 4 and 5 of VI 1912; GA 199, 8 and 11.IX.1920; GA 233a, 13 I 1924; GA 322, 1 X 1920.

[12] Steiner, R. GA 307, 17. VIII. 1923 (evening).

[13] Steiner, R. GA 26, 16. XI. 1924.

Michael-impulse leads the human being to the creative word, the Logos, the source of the "eternal poem"[14] of the world. We have every reason to take the words of the poet — "eternal poem" — seriously.

"Poem" means something we find: written and completed. In the form in which it is given it no longer changes; this must by no means be understood in the sense that it could not be transformed: it can certainly be altered by the way in which it is understood and conceived. "Eternal poem," therefore, has a double meaning: on the one hand, that the poem has been given since eternity, on the other hand, that, for the perceiving human, its meaning will forever change.

But "poem" also means that the text is not only addressing thinking, but mainly feeling, cognizing feeling. Therefore, the emphasis is on "warmth" and "feeling," "love for Nature," and "thinking-of-the-heart" in Steiner's Michael-letters:

> Michael frees the thoughts from the sphere of the head, opens their way to the heart and releases enthusiasm in the soul, so that the human being can live in the soul's dedication to everything that can be experienced in the ***light of thinking***. The Michael-age has begun. Hearts begin to have thoughts, enthusiasm no longer streams from mystical darkness only, but from a clarity of the soul which is carried by thought.[15]

In Michaelic living, thinking the cognizing feeling is covibrating. This is the thread on which thinking depends:

> .... even though the human being thinks with the head, the heart feels the light or darkness of thought....[16]

The Michael-impulse leads the human being to the wordless living thinking, which opens the ***warm*** understanding for Nature and the Cosmos. This living sphere makes it possible to begin the "reading" of creation, the body of the world distinct from the forces which created it. In relation to this sphere one begins to sense the Logos-nature of creation: that it is truly a poem, a condensation of sense, of meanings, a seed which can open as a new blossom in the human spirit. This is the unique newness in this world: the greatest possible contraction, condensation of the spiritual meaning of creation:

> And yet it is a world in itself,
> full of sweet and hidden, never witnessed sounds,
> endowed with its peculiar unharmed beauty,
> no-one's echo or reflection;
> and even if you'd learn to read therein,
> a book that you will never fathom.[17]

---

14 Hofmannsthal, Hugo von. ***Was ist die Welt?***

15 Steiner, R. GA 26, 17.VIII.1924

16 Steiner, R. GA 26, 16.XI. 1924

17 Hofmannsthal, ***Was ist die Welt?***

The Two Spiritual Worlds

The sun of creation, the Logos, pours itself out in the form of two spiritual streams. One is the stream of I-beings, hierarchies which themselves undergo a development according to their own free will, always inspired from above, by higher beings, ultimately by the Logos.[18] The other stream is the body of the world, which has its foundation in the highest hierarchies, and ultimately in the Logos. The body of the world is now detached from the creative forces ("poem"), and is maintained by Nature-spirit-beings which substitute the original hierarchical beings. At the end of both streams we find the human being participating in both: in the upper stream of I-beings through his spiritual part, in the lower stream of the world's bodily nature through his inherited organism.

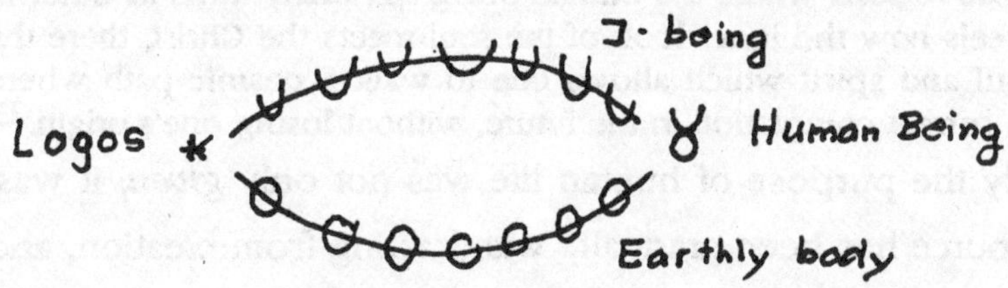

The relationship of the human being to these two spheres is also twofold. Our access to the hierarchies is through our superconscious levels which participate with their sphere. But our every-day consciousness is separated from this super-conscious sphere by an abyss,[19] which is inhabited by the beings of our sub-conscious. When we rise from the every-day-level of consciousness — in a creative moment, or in meditation — the Logos-spark "in the flesh,"[20] taking our departure point from the every-day consciousness, allows us to unite our every-day I (Ego) with the true I in the super-conscious sphere.

Among I-beings, only the human being has access to the bodily part of the world; it integrates the two worlds and keeps them united. We are united with the bodily aspect of the world through sense-perception which is now interwoven with analytical conceptualities unsuitable to understand Nature and the Cosmos. But through the percept, which is always accessible, and always given, we are in contact with the outer side of the cosmic text. It is only an exception that — in art and religious life — the inner source of thoughts, of creative ideas are accessible to us.

---

[18] GA 26, 19.X.1924: "In the ancient past, man saw divine-spiritual beings when he turned his inner look in the direction where his own thoughts reveal themselves today."

[19] Kühlewind, Georg. *Das Licht des Wortes*. chapter: "Die Struktur der Bewußtseinsseele." Stuttgart, Germany: Verlag Freies Geistesleben. 1984.

[20] Kühlewind, Georg. *Die Erneuerung des Heiligen Geistes*. Chapter: "Die Fleischwerdung." Stuttgart, Germany: Verlag Freies Geistesleben. 1992.

Thus — in the super-conscious sphere — the human being is in touch with two spiritual worlds: one is the sphere of the hierarchies from where we enter earthly life at birth, and where we return at the time of death. The other we find through their *expression* in the fabric of the sense-perceptual world.[21] We find access to these two spheres through two impulses: the Christ-impulse leads directly to the inner source, Michael to the spirituality of the cosmos. The latter impulse can be understood as a differentiation of the Christian path in our time.

> Michael will give the correct orientation when we deal with the world which surrounds us in thinking and acting. To Christ we will have to find the way inside ourselves.
>
> Since the time of the mystery of Golgatha the human soul has the possibility to reach the Christ.[22]
>
> In those regions where the human being spiritually turns its outer look to Michael, and feels how the inner look of the soul meets the Christ, there thrives the surety of soul and spirit which allows one to walk a cosmic path where one will find one's correct completion in the future, without losing one's origin.[23]

Originally the purpose of human life was not only *given;* it was also readable.[24] As the Divine source has been gradually withdrawing from creation, and as the bodily aspect of the world has become a more or less calculable *work,* the readability has been more and more lost. But "work" is still pointing to creator-beings, as a "work of art" is pointing to its master. But readability — in fact even the idea that, in principle, Nature should be understandable or readable — was entirely lost in the latter half of the nineteenth century, when the view of Nature as "work" turned into the lower conception of Nature as "things." A *thing* is no longer pointing to an artist (a metaphor used by Thomas Aquinas) but at best to a craftsman, who does not intend to *say* something through his product. A *thing* can also come about *by accident*, and thus we find today the "primal bang" as the accepted beginning of everything (including the human being).

> One no longer saw a Divine-Spiritual work in the forms of Nature, but something without spirit, of which one nevertheless claimed that it produced the spirit in which the human being lives.[25]

The world has lost its "poem-nature." The initially given meaning, the great statement, which *was* the world, has become silent. Today it is obvious that this occurred in order to help the human being to come of age, to adopt responsibility for itself and for the world, to give new sense to a world void of meaning. The world, originally light, has become

---

21 Steiner, R. GA 199, 18.IX.1920 and 20.VIII.1920.

22 Steiner, R. GA 26, 2.XI.1924.

23 Steiner, R. GA 26, 9.XI.1924.

24 Steiner, R. GA 26, 25.I.1925.

25 Steiner, R. GA 26, 14.XII.1924.

dark. Next to the altogether unreadable Nature we have cluttered the world with "utility-objects," which do not speak, do not serve expression or conversation. This mute, lightless world can now be illumined anew by the human being, because of the spark of the Logos which is carried within. The world can again be made into a poem, a new one.

> Humanity will integrate itself into the development of the world. The Divine-Spiritual, where the human originates, can — as cosmically expanding humanity — illumine the cosmos which now exists as a mere copy of the Divine-Spiritual.
>
> What will light up through humankind is no longer identical with that which once existed as cosmos. By going through humanity the Divine-Spiritual will experience a nature which it did not manifest before.[26]

[26] Steiner, R. GA 26, 25.X.1924.

THE SUBSTANCE OF THE I

Two of the more typical questions of natural science are: "Of what?" and "Why?" It is characteristic for both that they do not allow a final answer — one can continuously repeat the question. Also, such questions are always hiding their own source: the I. For questions can only be asked by an I-being, out of its own beginning, its original initiative. If the answer refers to an I-being one can no longer ask "Why?" — no answer could be satisfactory;[1] and just with respect to the I the question "of what?" is impossible, since every answer would not refer to the I itself, only to the appearing part or "sign" of the I, by means of which it is articulating itself within the sense-perceptual world. Here the essence of the I is in touch with the essence of the word.

What does a word consist of? One understands quickly that there is no answer to this question because it could only respond to the carrier of the word: longitudinal air-waves, paper and ink, leather, the parts of a clay-tabloid where the clay is carved out, etc. The word as such has no "substance," it is a pure "configuration" or "constellation;" in the sense of informations- or communications-theory it is an "improbability in the arrangement of carrier-substances" — which could be *any* substance.

In this context one has to notice that the degree of improbability is by no means sufficient to determine the word. If a typewriter has 100 signs, the accidental probability that a word such as "Faust" will appear is $1:100^5$; but equally large is the possibility for the word "gsidy," which comes about if one consistently types the adjacent letters to the right of f-a-u-s-t, and this is the case with any combination of 5 signs, e.g., "Fffff." Only an I-being that knows or creates meaning independent of the degree of probability is able to determine whether an improbable combination is even making sense.

The essence of the word is independent of the carrier that helps the word to appear in the sense-perceptible world. However, one might have certain doubts as to whether a pure configuration could exist without a carrier, although it can be found in the source of the *appearing* configuration. A text or a form (e.g. the form of a seal) first emerges within

---

* Translation: Friedemann Schwarzkopf. from
Kühlewind, Georg. *Die Substanz des Ich*. unpublished German Manuscript.

20465 Placer Hills Road, Colfax, CA 95713
1 Note by the Translator: for if an I-being *begins* without being compelled within a chain of cause and effect, it in itself is the responsible cause.

the spirit or consciousness of a human being and then it can be transferred to a material carrier. Brain-research demonstrates that the processes in the central nervous system are not *depicting*; i.e., neither a perceptual image or fantasy picture, nor a text or thought are encoded in the brain in a form that would *correspond* to its source in a way that it could be re-translated. But if it would exist in the brain in a picturing fashion, the question would merely be postponed: how did the formation come into the brain? Therefore, one can say with certainty, that a "configuration" which appears at a later stage in some form within the sense-perceptual world is first originating without a carrier, without substance.

As a result of growing insight into the mechanism of the brain, in order to explain the phenomena of consciousness — especially the *attention* — science finds itself forced to assume a principle that is *independent* of this mechanism as well as of any sort of matter: a "self" that directs the mechanism of the brain. This cannot be localized in the brain; on the contrary, this would be the entity that determines which consciousness-function and which corresponding brain-mechanism — localizable in a specific area of the brain — is to be effective, or which part of the perceptual image is important, or where the boundaries of the perceived details have to be found etc.

Thus we are again confronted with the activity of the human I, for only the *human* attention is free, i.e., not determined according to the species. Freedom means the independence of an I-being: only *someone* can be free, i.e., *begin*, initiate a chain of causes, without having to be himself predetermined by a cause. Freedom of one's doing begins with the freedom of the attention.

The human being can direct its attention at random. But a question is raised as to how long its attention is able to remain with its object. To the animal the attentional sphere is "given," and it cannot abandon this sphere. The attention of the adult is *intentional*, i.e., always directed to "something." *Something* means: conceptual outline.[2] The attention can only select a "something," or a "that," if the selection is *repeatable*, like the possibility to remember and to recognize a phenomenon. When an object of nature is concerned, the conceptual "outline" has the form of our representation of the respective phenomenal element, since we do not know the true ideas of the phenomena of nature. Or, in other words, the *names* of the objects of nature are not signs for an *understanding*, but refer to their *characteristic attributes*. Man-made objects on the other hand are normally recognized and identified by their *functional* concept or intention.

In both cases the intentional attention is already conceptually formed. This means that the attention of the little child cannot be intentional before it learns to speak ("speech" in the largest sense of the word), because the conceptualities are given with the language

[2] Note by the Translator: that it is identifiable by conceptually delineated elements.

and thus grasped by the consciousness. Just because the attention of the little child is still entirely *receptive* and not *grasping* — not directed upon something — but also not yet divided between world and one's own sensation, the miracle of learning to speak and think can come about. For this end the attention must be able to grasp *simultaneously* the outer perceptual side and the inner aspect of the speaking gesture, its sense or meaning. For instance, already at a very early age the glance of the mother is answered. The two looks meet: this first conversation (impossible between man and animal) is still independent of the mother-tongue — a single "glance of a moment" in the development of human consciousness. This is followed by mutual smiling, still independent of language. The "inner side" of these speaking gestures can hardly be expressed in any "word"-language; but no one will doubt that they have "meaning." In this "exchange," perceiving and thinking are not yet divided; this kind of perceiving-thinking is not the perceiving and thinking of the adult, neither their simple addition, but something of a qualitatively different nature. It is similar to an earlier evolutionary stage of mankind when perception and thinking remained undivided, far into the time of the development of sounding speech.

With the integration of conceptualities, the attention of the child becomes more and more intentional, i.e., directed at a definite "something," and the non-intentional, receptive attention is less and less involved, except for the perception of *new* conceptualities. For that task, even the adult has only this kind of attention: neither can it be directed at "*that,*" a something that is not yet understood, nor to something else — for in that case it could not behold the *new*.

The phenomena of speech — in the above characterized wider sense — can manifest only among human beings because they always require that a sign of the perceptual world is "understood." Originally understanding is always intuitive, i.e., unreduceable to something else, like habit, usage, some kind of mechanism, etc. This applies also to the adult when he perceives a thought that is *new* to him: the perceptual signs — the words for instance — are not new, only their inner aspect; the intuition by the I is required in order to understand them.

In the child's intuition, and in the rare moments when the adult is understanding something new, we find a non-intentional attention. For the period when the child is learning to speak, when its receptive attention is most active, it is easy to see that I-consciousness is not yet present, even though the "learning" of speaking and thinking is an eminent I-activity. The I-like free attention is present — because the faculties of speaking and thinking are not inherited — but the consciousness of the self emerges much later. In the adult one can observe a similar paradox in the phenomenon of the surrendering attention in perceiving or thinking, and specifically by self-observation in retrospect: while my attention is living in complete surrender the self-consciousness is submerged. The I-consciousness awakens when the attention encounters itself — *only* attention can meet itself. The small child does not have this faculty, because the possibility of *reflection* — that the attention or consciousness can look upon itself — is surfacing only at the developmental stage of the constellation of the consciousness-soul. In the adult the strong attentional intensity — which is *given* to the child — has to be established by a schooling of consciousness or an artistic training in a specific discipline. Both these phenomena demonstrate that the presence of the real I has to be seen on the one hand as a surrendering attention; on the other hand it can be experienced super-consciously and dreamlike, in the child as well as the adult.

What does attention consist of? Since it is either intentionally directed upon something or receptively adopting an idea into itself, it must consist of the same "substance" as the word or the idea: pure potential to configure. The attention can assimilate any constellation into itself. When one says: "the attention is directed upon something," it means that this "something" has been received into the attention. If it concerns the configuration of a phenomenon of the sense-perceptible world, the attention becomes identical with the *image* of the thing — the representational picture — and becomes *knowledge*. If it concerns the configuration of the *idea* of the respective object, the attention adopts the form (or constellation) of the idea. In this case the thing becomes transparent for the knower, transparent to his attention: permeable. This is the *understanding*, which constitutes *cognition*. That which is formed in the idea or a word is subject to the human spirit — the I-being in its unformed state — which is free and open to be configured: this is the human attention. Its substance is the same as that of the idea.

Since the middle-ages the expression of "substance" has undergone an essential transformation: downwards, as it happened to so many other words. In Scholasticism, and for Dante still, "substance" stood for hierarchical being, angels, archangels, cherubim, seraphim, etc., i.e., understanding beings:

> "These *substances,* since they first had joy therein,
> On God's face have their constant vision kept,
> Wherefrom nothing is hidden or unseen."
>
> Dante, Paradiso XXIX,76

Later, "substance" meant the being or essence of a thing. Today the word has a meaning contrary to the original: "Substance" is the answer to the question "Of what?", therefore exactly that which is not the configuration, not understandable, not understanding. The

English word "understand" corresponds directly to the Latin verb "substare," of which the present tense participle is "substans." In many languages "understanding" is expressed by a modification of the verb "standing," for example, in Greek (epistasthai).

The intentional attention — directed to something — is a preparation for understanding; this comes about at the moment when the grasping attention turns into a receiving attention without diminishing its intensity and concentratedness in the process. Only what is conceptual, ideal, is understandable. But one should not conceive these expressions in too narrow a sense. We can speak about musical ideas, or ideas in painting, and the even higher ideas of the world of nature.

Attention seems to be a bridge between the one who is attentive and the object of attention. Observing it more accurately, one notices that the "witness" who is attentive cannot be aware of himself when he is intensely observing — in full surrender; if he would do this, his attention would wander from the object to himself as another object. In both cases the subject remains hidden and untraceable because it is always where the attention is most intensive. The subject becomes identical with the object of attention. The one who is attentive cannot be distinguished from his attention. (One cannot speak about an ***attentive*** one, when he is not attentive.) He is given — to the extent of full identity — to the object of attention. The human I exists in its functioning, i.e., in its surrender; it has no static existence. It only *is* in doing, in activity, in becoming — "becoming-that;" properly speaking one should not designate it by a noun, rather by a verb. In this respect it is participating in the way in which hierarchical beings *exist* who are also identical with their respective task, their doing. Therefore, the human I *is* in loving, creating, in surrender and attention. It consists of thinking, feeling and willing attention. Self-encounter is possible only for the I-like attention, for a self. It is known that only an I-being can recognize its own mirror-image, whereas animals are reacting — if they do — in a totally different manner. However, the human being normally mistakes its reflection — the sensation of the self — for its I, confounds that which is felt with the one who feels.

The human being as I-being *is* wherever its attention is. If it is with its bodily sensation, the I is attached to it: in the New Testament this attachment is called *"the Flesh."* When this attachment becomes permanent, the autonomy, the freedom of attention, is lost; it is divided mainly between the self-sensing and the world. The self-experience branches out into various more or less independent pieces of attention which make up the psychological *Subconscious*. But it is also dispersed between the countless learned concepts and representations. In the first place the schooling of consciousness has the task to re-establish the autonomy and undividedness of the attention. In our times this is a schooling of the thinking, feeling and willing attention.

THE FORCE OF THE LOGOS AND THE FORCE OF THE "I"

"When someone says: 'I have been wounded,' he must use the word 'I' in a sense which is comprehensible to others, for instance in the sense of 'the one who is now speaking to you'...." This is how the mathematician and logician Gottlob Frege[1] is uniting the two realities: the I and the speaking. In the mentioned case it is I who is speaking. The one who speaks is an I, and the speaker means himself, as the one who speaks, when he uses the little word "I." This small word refers so radically and entirely to itself, that it can be used only with respect to myself. It is basically not a noun — even though it is often used in that way — but a personal pronoun. This case of extreme "self-meaning" has only one parallel: the word "word." Like the word "I," it points in a similar way to itself. However, there are many words, and there are many speakers, who are justified to say "I;" therefore they have to say "I" and have to speak. And although there is a multitude of words, every single one means only itself, nothing "else" — in contradiction to what is generally believed. Every word says "I" in its own way.

1. The Basic Phenomena of Language

Self-meaning

It is not difficult to see that the sounds of language do not mean anything but themselves; although one is often tempted to characterize them — mostly in a poetic sense — one can never exhaust their potential. Even with regard to conjunctions, prepositions and many adjectives (e.g., "although," "in," "beautiful"), it is easy to see that they signify a specific understanding or gesture of consciousness, not something that would be sense-perceptible. Yet this is in no way different from nouns and verbs, which

---

* Translation from German manuscript, *Logoskraft und Ichkraft*, Friedemann Schwarzkopf;

20465 Placer Hills Road, Colfax, California 95713, USA.
also in: *Journal for Anthroposophy*. Fall 1990 No 51, pp. 70-79 and Spring 1991 No 52, pp. 46-57. Dripping Springs, Texas: Anthroposophical Society.

[1]G. Frege, ***Logische Untersuchungen***, Vandenhoeck & Ruprecht, Göttingen, 1966; G. Kühlewind, *Becoming Aware of the Logos*, Chapter *The Speaker*, Lindisfarne Press, West Stockbridge, Mass. 1984.

are seemingly designating a perception. "Table" means every table as function, independent of size, material, number of legs (a cloth can serve as table even when it is placed on a sloping meadow) because it means ***my understanding*** of "what a table is," nothing else. The child that has acquired this understanding will recognize everything that is "tabling" as table. Man-made things are in principle understandable, i.e., truly comprehensible, thus real (=effective) concepts, "real essences" in the sense of John Locke. For modern man, this is different with regard to the designations of nature. "Rose" means certain perceptible characteristics which allow us to recognize or name the thing. If the number of petals of calyx or blossoms, or the amount of stamens, or the form of leaves do not coincide, we know from ***that***, that we are not dealing with the same species. In this case understanding means: "something that appears in a certain way, is called a rose," or a rose looks like ***that***; this corresponds to the "nominal essences" of Locke. With verbs it is similar. In any case the word means my understanding. In slightly different terms this coincides with Wittgenstein's view about the meaning of words.

This elucidates that the problem of the "generality" of the concept and the singularity of the individual object of perception exists only for the naive consciousness which is not aware of its own role. We perceive the individual as being a single entity, only when we relate it to the universal of which it is a specification. No object is green, large, or round "in general," but shows a shade of green, a certain size and a specific roundness.

Energetics

This touches upon the "energetic" (Wilhelm von Humboldt) role of language: language does not "name" something that would somehow exist even without a concept or some understanding of the place of the identified individual within the context or structure of the given entirety of the world. It's primary function is basically the individualizing of distinguishable entities by means of conceptual outline, which is provided by the language — always, whether one deals with real or nominal essences. In this sense Th. Georgiades[2] speaks of "naming": language "names" and creates in this way the elements of the outer and inner world. Its structure is articulated especially through grammar, which provides the consciousness with the respective categorial context.

For the child, the world is created through the language even today: at that stage of the development of consciousness, word and concept are not yet separated. Initially the individual human being — also mankind — thinks in language, and by means of language. Later it learns from the language how to articulate in a structured manner and abstract thinking develops independent of language and words, a thinking that is also

[2]Georgiades, Th., ***Nennen und Erklingen***, Chap. III, Vandenhoek & Ruprecht, Göttingen, 1985.

capable of conceiving concepts which are not provided by the language; those are the scientific and technical concepts.

The Not-natural Origin of Language

The self-meaning of the words and the structure of the world emerge from within the language; because language itself does not consist of elements which are given by nature: neither words nor grammar can be found in nature. Even where language is imitating the sounds of nature, it uses its own palette of sounds which is independent of nature (for the barking of dogs Wau-Wau, Bow-Wow or Gaf-Gaf). There is no natural or general connection between the form of a sound and the meaning of a word, and there are no sounds which two or several languages would have in common. In the Maori language the mother is called "papa," in the Georgian language the father is called "mama."

A Language has to work with its own specific means; those are not "found" since the means which nature could provide would have to be first assigned by the language, in order to become "something" — the *what* or conceptual outline. Only through language are such elements individualized out of the Given: namely, according to the structure and lexicon of the language.

Although the language is *given*, to the child — the human being is not forming or creating it — it is not given as a process of nature but through the human environment. Since thinking is born out of the faculty of speaking, thinking is not inherited either; and neither is the ability to perform consciously intended formed movements. All of these specifically human faculties are a *super-conscious* predisposition of the human being; they are a *faculty* without the conscious awareness of how they are performed. We do not know how we produce sounds, we do not speak our mother-tongue by grammatical knowledge, and we do not know *how* we are thinking. Likewise we do not know how we are looking at other human beings, how we are smiling, or how we perform other articulated gestures: all of this is part of language.

Two-fold Aspect of Language

All the elements of human language have two aspects: a sense-perceptible, "appearing" part (acoustically or visually perceptible), and a hidden, non-appearing part, the meaning or sense; both live within the consciousness where they can be recalled. The perceptible *sign* lies on the level of the every-day consciousness; the meaning and its *understanding* is super-conscious. These two levels are separated by an abyss; only a shadow — a reflection — or the result of understanding, the understood, is reaching *this* side of the abyss. Thus language and the word are becoming a very important bridge across the abyss — or connection between the two levels of consciousness — if they are *fully* conceived and spoken with inner participation, not merely outer attention. On one side is the acoustic sign; its meaning is on the other. The perceptible side is discontinuously structured, the other side, understanding is much more continuous. One can count the sounds, words and sentences, but not the number of understandings along the text; those are rather flowing from one into the other. This also characterizes the specific way and manner in which something is structured and articulated from within the Logos-sphere: language and thinking. Words and concepts are distinct from one another, and at the same time united within a word-system, or conceptual system. There is no such thing as a *single* word outside of the entirety of language, no *single* concept without a conceptual system. In fact, the distinction occurs just because of the inner connectedness within the conceptual sphere, i.e., in the hidden part of language. A concept lives by the grace of adjoining concepts with which it is connected and from which it is distinguished *simultaneously*; and at *the same time* it is helping its adjoining concepts to exist as individual concepts in themselves. The same can be said about words: they are *wording* only in the context of speaking, even if this should include non-verbal elements like gestures, intonation and facial expression.

In language and thinking, *distinguishing* and *connecting* are one. If this oneness is given up, we lose the Logos-sphere and enter a field of disconnected piecework, an unstructured world where everything — what? — is flowing together. This is just the nature of words and concepts that they consist of these two gestures at the same time: *separating* and *connecting*; if they are performed separately, for themselves, they represent the domains of the two adversary forces.

Transparency

One can directly and immediately understand one's own thinking and concepts; they *are* understanding — that is the meaning of direct immediacy. When one contemplates the self-meaning, one experiences the evidence that such understanding is always referring to itself: it understands itself. It is a creation. Wherever an "otherness" appears, there is not-understanding, and just that is the "other." In the perceptual world there is only one phenomenon we can likewise understand immediately: that is language. This includes the arts which also have a verbal structure similar to language because they too consist of sense-perceptible signs full of meaning — even if this "meaning" cannot be rendered by thinking, or through concepts of the usual kind. The perceptible signs are transparent for an appropriate understanding within thinking, or within feeling, as in the arts. The elements of language are seed-like: any concept can be a departure point for growth. It can be pursued in all directions according to its connection with other concepts: horizontally-sideways, or vertically-upwards to its primal meaning, which allows for any possible application, also future uses, or enlargements of the present meaning. One can also do this with words of a language; but there the way in which the words are supposed to appear is prescribed by syntax and grammar, whereas the meaning behind the sign is allowed to change. The growth and life of such conceptualities is also a specific potential of the higher ideas - "feelable ideas" — in art, music, painting, sculpture, etc. — as well as in nature. An example for the latter is Goethe's idea of the archetypal plant. Nature is like a letter or sign for mightier, "feelable," and willing ideas, formations of feeling and willing, in the same way as our normal, familiar ideas are thought formations as well. The "feelability" of the ideas of nature appears in their perceptibility; every one of our senses is open to feeling; for instance, a hearing sense in music, a seeing sense in painting, a tasting sense for the wine expert. Every nature-phenomenon is so strongly willed in its specific qualities — *being thus* — that human will is comparatively powerless. One can only allow one's own attentional will to be imprinted by the "suchness" of the perception; the more one is able to do this, the more one's perception is precise and rich.

The construction of a sentence displays a hierarchical structure. The sounds surrender their individual character to the word, and the words do the same within a sentence, which assigns them their specific meaning by reducing their many possibilities; the meaning of entire sentences is also specified through the context of the text and situation in which they are spoken, possibly serving a higher meaning within a paragraph, etc.

It is possible to determine whether or not one is dealing with a text, even if one is unable to decipher the writing. In a writing one finds phonological, grammatical and syntactical regularities, i.e., an irregular repetition of elements. Regularity would point to an ornamental character as in a carpet. Although natural science finds regularities in nature, the elements are never strictly evenly repeated. Therefore, one can know that nature has the character of a text. Higher — living, feeling, willing — ideas would be necessary to understand this text, and the ability to work with such ideas.

"That" and the Witness

As soon as a *that* is appearing on the horizon of consciousness — whether it is something really understood or something nominally defined by its outer appearing form, as long as it can be can be remembered at will (a reaction upon a familiar sign could also be a reflex) — one cannot separate this event from the presence of a witness. A *that* exists *for* an I, because it is conceptually outlined; even if the I is not aware of this if the

I-consciousness is not awake at the same time. This means that the I is already participating in the selection and formation of a distinct entity, a ***that***. As soon as the Given is differentiating itself into distinct entities, the I is participating in this process — depending on its actual abilities — under the guidance of its conceptual system and intuitional faculty. This relates also to the way thought intuitions or perceptions are received. Concerning a demanding text or perception of an art piece the participation of the recipient is usually conscious, however, much less in ordinary perception. The hidden part of the outer signs of any language is only accessible to an I-being. Only an I-being is able to bring forth new meaning.

Because of the fact that sense, meaning and Logos-nature reveal themselves in sense-perceptible signs, one can say: "Only in the word has the spiritual world descended to the physical world."[3] This does not mean certain specific words, but the ability *for* the word or the ability to give meaning, the faculty to produce or understand new ideas and their signs.

2. The Word-nature of the Human Being

One who can understand a text, is also able to produce it; otherwise, one could not speak about understanding. ***Understanding*** has to be clearly distinguished from "reacting," which does not require understanding. The test for understanding is always something that is new to the one who is supposed to understand, especially since the new sense has to appear in already existing old words; it would not support understanding to invent new words. The understanding I is capable of finding or attributing new content or meaning in the familiar signs, thus "making unlimited use of limited means" (W.v. Humboldt). One can probably see this as the fundamental characterization of the I, by adding that the I is also able to produce new ideas out of itself, and to express them in old words. In this way one can picture the I as infinitely capable of articulating itself: on the one hand, in being able to touch and assume the form of every thought, even new ones, and on the other, in its creative activity, as source for new thought formations or, in the arts, new forms of feeling.

Neither the new understanding, nor the creation of new understandings can be ascribed to the sense-perceptible organism because this — as a biological-physical-chemical system endowed with a sensitive organization — has not the slightest inclination or capacity to conceive or produce new meaning. *Sense* means ***improbability***; however,

[3]R.Steiner, GA 96, 19.X.1906.

not every improbability makes sense. To evaluate *this*, is not possible for a sense-perceptible system which has to be a statistically causal determined system: nothing principally new can proceed from such a system. And if an accidental production were to take place, which instance would evaluate its truth, novelty, correctness, etc.? Rather, the sense-perceptible organism is analogous to the appearing part of the word, its sound-formation, whereas the invisible meaning of the word *happens* in that part of the human being which is not sense- perceptible either: because this meaning is a process as is the understanding. The sense *is* or *becomes* within understanding, indeed, it itself is understanding. This part of the human being is its I-being, which articulates itself within the organism as a means of expression. This is the part where the resourcefulness of the human being has to be found, the source of new ideas, new speech, new understanding. In this sense one has to adjust Frege's sentence: That which is wounded is the organism; that which is "now speaking" is the higher or true I, which is speaking without doubt *through* the organism.

The every-day I is a part of the true I which has identified itself with the organism; it is a shadow of the true I, and experiences itself in and through the organism. When one says "I," one normally points to the organism: an erroneous gesture because for the true I one has to look in the direction of the "pointer," not the "pointed;" and the pointer or speaker are not in the organism, in fact, not even in space, since he can only use the spatial as a means of expression. The I that has identified itself with the organism in a self-sensing gesture is not-speaking and not-cognizing. While alive, it can emancipate itself from this identification only by way of a schooling of consciousness, self-education.

These two I-beings are in touch with one another. Certain faculties of the true I — which are super-conscious for the every-day I — can also be performed by this every-day I, like thinking, speaking, or articulated bodily movements; these are faculties specific to the I, all acquired from the true I during childhood in the experience of the organism, before the lighting-up of the I-consciousness. During our every-day consciousness we do not know how we perform these activities, or how we direct our attention to any object in thinking and perceiving.

The connection between the two I-beings is not conscious, otherwise those faculties would be conscious, too; the I-beings are separated by an abyss — discontinuity — in the consciousness. The bridge across this abyss is the word. But this is also the bridge between you and me, between man and Godhead, between man and world. One can show that all these separations are caused by the same rift.

That part of the I-being that is analogous to the meaning of a word — which does not appear in the world of the senses, is liberated from the organism through death.

> "Now try to imagine that what man is expressing, what is flowing into the fleeting word, would be a 'self-uttering' of the human being, its essence and its revelation at the same time — then you find the way in which human beings meet each other in the middle between death and new birth. Word meets another word, the articulated word encounters an articulated word, an inwardly enlivened word meets the inwardly enlivened word. The human beings themselves are the words, and their sounding-together is the symphony of the articulated Word-being. In this sphere human beings live together without untransparency: they are truly living with one another, and one word, which is one human being, merging with the other word, the other human being. Here the karmic connections are formed which continue to work into the next life on earth; they manifest themselves in such a way that the human beings feel sympathy and antipathy, as it were, when they meet and encounter one another. This feeling is a reflection of the way in which human beings have addressed themselves in the spiritual world, in the middle between death and new birth. This is how we have spoken with one another — we, who were speech ourselves, who are now finding ourselves on earth again, in the shadowy reflection of this feeling."[4]

The not-natural, spiritual part is "permeable," directly understandable, like a thought; the body causes the characteristic of untransparency for everything sense-perceptible, except for the phenomena of speech. The body could be a pure expression of the true I, like the relation between sign and meaning of the word. Due to the natural needs of the body, not penetrated by the true I, and because of the formation of the every-day I, the structure of the human being deviates from that ideal.

Among the soul-functions, the purest effect of the true I can be found in thinking and perceiving and those activities which are guided by thinking. Therefore, the strength of the I can be measured by the degree of the pure energy of thinking, the ability for conceptual structuring: how articulate, and how high a rung it is reaching in the ladder of ideas.

Human freedom is based on the resourcefulness of the spirit. This can make beginnings, i.e., *initiate* causal chains; such beginnings are not effects of earlier causes; they can also interrupt causal chains. Heraclitus ascribes this faculty to the *Logos* which is dwelling within the soul, "growing from out of itself." To this Logos the human being owes its predisposition for speech, and therewith all specifically human faculties and activities: as they are rooted in the higher spiritual man, the true I, none of these can be inherited.

Nature as perceptual world is the outer side of past Logos-creation. The spark of the Logos that lives within the human being nourishes its creatively individualized Logos-force. Between human beings it makes communication possible, and because of it the perceptual world is principally knowable. In the Middle-Ages, the light of the perceptual world used to be characterized in the sentence: "*omne ens verum*" — "everything that is, is

[4] R.Steiner, GA 231, 14.XI.1923; see also: GA 215, 9.IX.1922; GA 107, 6.X.1908; GA 218, 4.12.1922.

true": *true* in the sense that it is unconcealed or cognizable, knowable; and this meant being created by the Logos — through the word.

The egoity, the "flesh," is self-sensing, not cognizing, not speaking. This is the result of a development which begins with learning to speak, but is not caused by this. Learning to speak also includes communicating gestures, long before verbal speech. In speaking, the speaker — the higher human being, the true I — penetrates the speech-organism in a not self-sensing manner, i.e., unegoistically. It is a later perversion of speech if the speaker is enjoying himself in the process. Conversation can remain free of this self-indulgence and then it can become "more quickening than light."

As the individuality of words and concepts is secured by their interactive relationship and connectedness, as words have no reality if separated from the wholeness of their language, likewise human individuals together are forming humanity, a language whose hidden inner side is the Logos itself. As the spirit of a language is mirrored in every single one of its words that it enlivens, likewise a living spark of the Logos-fire is present within each human being: as its concealed star-like essence, its eternal name who it *is* in the spirit, which utters itself in the spiritual world. But together these words build the Logos-language — sublime above all sounding languages, and thus the whole and the individual are held together, making one another mutually necessary, in the same way as the words in language.

3. Conversation

Viel hat erfahren der Mensch.
Der Himmlischen viele genannt,
Seit ein Gespräch wir sind
Und hören voneinander.

Much has experienced mankind;
And named many heavenly ones,
Since conversation we are,
And able to hear from the other.[5]

For a child as well as for ancient mankind, language can only develop in a mutual spiritual-collective consciousness; every other explanation for the phenomena of speech already requires the faculty of thinking, thus a kind of "translation." But thinking is based

[5]Hölderlin, 3.version of his Christ-hymn "Versöhnender" or: "Die Friedensfeier" in: Hölderlin, Friedrich. *Sämtliche Werke und Briefe*. Bd.I. S. 1068. (also S.368) Darmstadt, Germany: Wissenschaftliche Buchgesellschaft, 1989.

on language: not only on its vocabulary, but mainly on the grammar which outlines the hidden logical structure and relationships. Distinct from living in a joint spiritual collective, the necessity to communicate through language makes the human being lonely, but individualizes it at the same time. With its hidden inner side, language reaches into a spiritual sphere which used to be collective, but is now increasingly individual; the form in which this inner aspect of language is "appearing" on the earth is the ***understanding***. Understanding gives the human being the possibility to participate in a sphere which is not merely personal, even after the separation from a mode of consciousness where mankind used to live in a participation of sensing and feeling with little emphasis on being individual. The "old" dreamlike participation is now substituted by language, which reflects a lighter level of consciousness. Instead of a joint consciousness it requires mutual attention, which is a certain effort for the I when it has to engage in conversation.

Language individualizes because it creates a situation where one has to make connections by means of a sense-perceptible system of signs: everybody can speak and think alone. The communion that was lost is reestablished by the word which is thriving between the partners of a conversation. The next effort of the I is that the one who speaks has to express what he wants to say, to sheathe, or "enchant" his speaking-intention — "***that,***" the meaning of his sentences, which never appears directly to the outer senses — in forms and words of the language; and in order to understand, the listener has to "disenchant" the enchanted from the sounding language. The proof for understanding is whether the listener is able to render what he perceived in "his own words." The "detour" through enchantment and disenchantment is the application and also an education of the force of the Logos within the I: to read new meaning from the old signs, to bring new meaning into the old signs. The later this is practiced in the individual's and mankind's development of consciousness, the less is the direct wordless understanding participating in the process and the more it is up to the force of the I to solve this task, which is quite different in most languages. The less structured a language (archaic languages), the more the inner activity has to be active. One can also say that the more the outer side of languages is differentiated (analytical languages), the less the conversation is supported by the immediacy of communication, which can still be found, even today, as a kind of telepathy among people who maintained their archaic forms of life.

The possibility to ***become*** the entirely individual source for the word and for ideas was given to mankind through Christianity, the incarnation of the Logos. In that process the Logos settled on both sides of the abyss, which separates the conscious from the super-conscious. This potential exists for every human being, independent of its religious denomination. The realization of this potential depends on the quality of one's self-contemplation, which is made possible just because of this constellation, a "two-track" soul-life between a conscious and a super-conscious part. The subconscious interferes with this development, retards and disturbs it. Due to the presence of the Logos within the "flesh" — that part of the soul which is otherwise attached in a self-indulging gesture to the sensation of the body — the individualization of the super-conscious sphere can begin: from below upwards, because of the connectedness of the two I-beings.

Conversation means an exchange of two "wording" ideal sources. As one can see by the present-day test wether or not understanding took place — rendering the content in one's "own words" — it is a pre-condition for conversation that the thinking is to a certain extent independent from language. Prior to the time of the consciousness-soul, conversation was more like a conversation of the gods; because it was given from the sphere which is now super-conscious, a sphere which used to reach in a dreamlike mood into the every-day consciousness, before the "abyss" opened.

In conversation one tries to unite with the other human being through the word; if one is not sure whether one has ***heard*** correctly, one can ask, "did you say ***this***: ..... ?" But ***this*** relates to the outer side of speech, which was sense-perceptually perceived; this can be clarified, doubts about correct perception can be resolved, which is of fundamental importance with respect to other perceptions, like nature for instance.[6] The *content* can only be communicated by trusting the word and the understanding of the human being; there are no outer sense-perceptual criteria for correct understanding. Even if I render what I have heard in my own words, the "yes" of my conversational partner now depends on whether *he* is understanding my words correctly, the way in which *I* meant them. Confidence in the word is necessary because the most basic words cannot be defined: we use them to define the next group of words, e.g., technical or scientific expressions.

When one observes two human beings in deep conversation, one sees how they perform a little dance, in their facial expressions and small movements: when the one is speaking in his way, the other will imitate him softly as he follows the expressions, thoughts and feelings of the first; then they change roles. A pendulum-swing of the soul happens in the rhythm of speaking-listening-speaking-listening, stretched out in time, because normally it alternates so rapidly that it is hardly possible to observe it.

In sense-perceptual perceiving, the attention is usually changing quickly from being surrendered to the perceived, to one's awareness of being with oneself; perception really happens in the first phase; the second phase registers, identifies, gives names, and categorizes the perceived conceptually. This is so habitual that one doesn't normally

[6]R.Steiner, GA 45, Anhang V.

distinguish the two phases; if the perceived is new — something "special" that evokes awe — then the pure perceptual act separates from the registration in thought. Different is the perception of art: there the attention remains in the activity of perceiving; all the more since here the ***understanding*** is already happening within perception as an intelligence; art is not perceived by thinking; it is not necessary since thinking is contained within the artistic feeling — hearing and seeing are carriers of this feeling.

The pendulum swing of the attention between surrender and being-with-oneself is at the same time an oscillation between true I and every-day I. Therefore, only the second phase is normally experienced in full awareness, the surrender is experienced in a more dreamy mood, a kind of "sleeping into" the perception. I see a tree — then I say to myself: a maple-tree. Due to the instruction of the senses these two gestures can coincide, then I immediately see the tree as a "maple," without experiencing the two phases separately. But in that case it is an ***informational*** perceiving, it reaches only the concept, the ***what***, the general, and I do not even see the tree in its individual characteristics; I would not be able to make an imaginative representation of it. That is the lowest level of perception.

Except for the perception of another human being, one encounters a ***finished*** world in sense-perception: nature has reached a certain accomplishment and does not produce anything principally new (for instance the "buildings" and nests of animals and insects have basically not changed for ages). Also the sense-perceptible part of man-made things (even works of art) consists of nature-given substance. But very light and mighty ideas — even though "finished" — are shining from this substance to man, who is not prepared to grasp or comprehend and understand them. Therefore, the perceptual world of nature is waiting for man to supply its true idea, nevertheless allowing itself to be perceptible ("Wahr-nehmung"), even though it is not understood.

In the same way in which the I can leave the every-day I in its surrender to perception, it can also release itself in the opposite direction, to thinking, within the inner sphere of the soul, without sense-perception. This is the gesture of meditation, whether it is a thought, a representational image, or a symbol. Here one does not find a ***finished*** world, one has to participate if an understanding of the meditational theme is to occur. One carefully approaches the inner source of the Logos within oneself, one's own ***beginning***, or true I. This sphere is not giving itself in a finished outlook, which is also the reason why this sphere is not shining in a sense-perceptible fashion for given sense-organs. In this sphere the surrender only reaches the individually appropriate conscious level. Therefore, perception can be regarded as a continuous invitation for meditation because we do not have the appropriate ideas; in fact, on the level of our every-day perception we are even laming our perception[7] to mere informational perception in the extreme case.

In both pendulum swings from the departure point of every-day consciousness to perceiving on the one hand and intuitive understanding on the other, the ***receptive*** attention is activated. On the highest level of the every-day consciousness, where it is free, independent or autonomous, we find the possibility for ***intentional*** attention. With this attention — directed upon "something" — one begins one's self-education in order to metamorphosize the intentional into a receptive attention at the next stage; this can happen when the waking consciousness is no longer in need of finished conceptualities. Thus, one can say that the receptive attention is continuously at work in the activity of perceiving — in the rain of higher ideas — except for mere informational attention.

The attention of the human being is its true I, the star of the soul. As long as this living, feeling and willing attention does not behold itself the human being does not experience its ***I-am*** on a level of reality, but merely as a mirror-image; in our every-day I, we treat the attention as a faculty of man. Yet, what we ***are*** in the spirit, appears as a faculty on earth; likewise, the faculty for the word is like a shadow of our existence before birth or after death. Ultimately, ***attention*** is the essential human being.

The way in which divine beings exist can be characterized by two essential qualities. It consists of ***giving***, and since "having" is unknown in the heavenly world, it is a giving-of-oneself. The togetherness of divine beings is a ***mutual interpenetration*** of conscious beings, where one is within the other without losing its individuality. For the spiritual existence of man these two characteristics are equivalent to the "uttering-of-oneself," the sounding-together, the merging of one word within the other. On earth the giving-of-oneself corresponds to the giving of attention, and what one ***is*** in conversation together with another human being. The elevated given attention is called surrender or love. In conversation, this pendulum-swing of the souls re-establishes the communion in an earthly way.

The listening to the speaking of another human being is in the ideal case a pendulum-swing of surrender — of receptive attention — in two directions: one tries to make one's own thinking as silent as possible and allows the ***thinking*** of the other to think within oneself; but one also ***perceives*** the other in his facial expression, his gestures, glance, sound of the voice and presence. The presence of the one who speaks increases, the more he speaks from a source of intuition, the "here and now," the less he is speaking from memory or memorized understanding. The presence — one can also call it extended spiritual presence, a force which streams through sensible-supersensible

[7]R.Steiner, GA 21, I.; GA 188, 10.I.1919; GA 198, 10.VII.1920; GA 153, 11.IV.1914.

perception — helps one to understand what is spoken; one may think of certain kinds of lectures where immediate full understanding comes about, which is afterwards — without one's own doing — plunging into deep forgetting. One should compare this to a read *lecture*, or a tape where perhaps the same text is given, however, without presence.

After having perceived the talking of the other, it is good — in a healing conversation — to allow it to ring forth in a pause of silence: *only* then should one reconsider the content a-new and prepare the answer — if necessary — ideally from one's improvising presence.

The structure of the ideal conversation shows that in conversation one can only give or be given: one cannot *take*. This outlines an entirely unegoistic model for human behavior. This is partly practiced in the Holy Communion: there one *receives* the nourishment, one does not take it; it is likewise exemplified in the image of the feeding of the five thousand and four thousand (Matth. 14:13-21, 15:32-39; Mark 6:31-34, 8:1-10; Luke 9:10-17; John 6:1-15.) where the nourishment is also *offered*. This model should be effective in the social-economic life. Steiner's "fundamental social law" is a model for the structure of conversation.[8]

Conversation should also be practiced with regard to nature: there the primal phenomena can be seen and understood at the same time, and the *taking* from nature can be redeemed by doing it in understanding her appropriately — which is still practiced by Indian tribes who live the traditional way.

In conversation, the individualizing effect of language is redeemed again. An articulated unity of free individuals arises: the human community, led together by the same language.

> "Denn der Geist, der uns vereinsamt, will
> völlig sicher sein, uns zu vereinen."
>
> "For the spirit that makes us lonely
> wants to be sure to re-unite us."[9]

---

[8]R.Steiner, GA 24, *Geisteswissenschaft und soziale Frage*:

"The welfare of a community of human beings working together is the greater, the less the individual is claiming the fruits of its work for itself, i.e., the more it is sharing such fruits with its co-workers, and the more its own needs are satisfied by the efforts of the others, and not its own."

also: "The healthy social life is found,
when in the mirror of each human soul
the whole community finds its reflection,
and when in the community the virtue of each one is living."

[9]Rilke, *Inschrift*, Werke. Auswahl in 2 Bänden, Insel Verlag 1957, p. 341.

4. But Soon we are a Ringing Song...

In the final version of his great hymn[10] Hölderlin repeats the earlier quoted thoughts in a slightly modified form and adds the words in the title of this chapter:

"Viel hat von Morgen an,
Seit ein Gespräch wir sind und hören voneinander,
Erfahren der Mensch; bald sind wir aber Gesang."

"Much has experienced mankind,
since conversation we are, and hear from each other,
for ages. But soon we are a singing song.

We will now try to understand the last sentence.

The seed of the Logos within the Human being — God's breath — is a driving force to creative activity. All I-beings have in common that they are never finished, they never reach accomplishment; all are in movement, on the way, in a life "from truth to truth," i.e., "from unconcealedness to unconcealedness."

The Logos is a formative force, creating meaning; this means the quintessence of all forms, pure forms, ideal forms, before they come to appearance within matter: like the "word of the heart" (Thomas Aquinas), not even sure in which language to appear.

In modern man, the force of the Logos allows for the immediacy of thinking and perceiving: two entirely different immediacies.

The possibility to *understand* one's own thinking directly is an inheritance from the primal revelation, a state of existence of "knowing transparency," the *vidya* of man. Understanding comes to the consciousness from the opposite direction than perception: As perception enters from "in front," thought intuitions are springing forth "from behind."

In the act of *perceiving* the receptive attention is directly given; but the ability to "read" this, the understanding of what is given by perception, is lacking; it is like a foreign language. The way in which perception is given is a kind of atavism or perhaps also a *gift*.

In *thinking*, man has to prepare the receptive gesture through the art of meditation — apart from the rare exceptions of *grace* which can happen independently of a prior removal of the obstacles. In any case the human being — as the receptive *chalice* — has an important role in the formation of ideas. The chalice has its own form, and therefore the chalice and the content which fills it, are assimilating themselves to one another. This is the grand idea of the *adaequatio* of Thomas Aquinas.

---

[10]Hölderlin, *Friedensfeier*.

The two areas, perceiving and thinking, are correlated. If the sense-organs are healthy, the result of perceiving — the *percept* — is determined by the way the attention is conceptually equipped, i.e., the quality of available conceptualities. These conceptualities are given by the intuitive receptive gesture of thinking. To what extent the perceptually given is "understood," how much it has received a merely preliminary structure as a result of inadequate concepts, and how far it is "dimmed down," depends on the quality or the kind of concepts.

If one treats language as an object of perception, it offers a large spectrum of understanding, from the informative to the artistic and to the meditative text. Perception of nature allows for identical given elements to have a similar manifoldness: from natural scientific calculation to the feeling of qualities (discovering the healing properties of plants, or technical accomplishments of the pre-scientific age — like "knowing" the statics of cathedral architecture without having "physics"), as far as the understanding of the union of nature and man: a high meditative level.

Since I-beings are never finished, and because man has "come of age" (by being able to reflect upon his own consciousness), it is now man's task to continue the work on his own development by himself, a task which was almost unknown to mankind. The next stage would be the experience of his own spiritual self, independent of the organism. Further stages would follow. These future steps are clearly envisioned in the tradition of Christianity. The first step is from the "righteous" or the "children of God" of the Old Testament to the sonhood or the "brothers of Christ." In the prologue of the John-Gospel the characterization of the "children of God" (John 1:12,13),[11] is followed by: "And the Logos was made flesh, and dwelt among us, and we beheld his radiance, a radiance as of the one-born son of the Father, full of grace and truth." In this way the theme of the ***flesh*** (the "children of God" could ***not*** be born from the will of the flesh, John 1:13)[12] is connected with the Logos, so that He could also become present on this side of the abyss. The result is the seeing of the radiance ("glory") from "face to face" (1.Cor. 13:12), in "unconcealedness" (literal translation of the Greek *A-letheia*, "Truth"), by going beyond the stage of the Old Testament, the seeing with a covered face. One becomes a Christian through the baptism with fire and the Holy Spirit; "and" does not mean a difference, but a oneness of the connected concepts (which happens quite often in the Bible). It refers to the fire of the Logos, in the sense of Heraclitus.

---

[11]"But to all who received Him, who believed in His name, He gave power to become *children* of of God; who were born, not of blood nor of the will of the flesh nor of the will of man, but of God."

[12]The King James version of the bible translates the Greek "tekna" with "sons," whereas the Standard Revised Version reads correctly: "children."

The following passages of the New Testament show the dimension of the ideas of early Christianity:

> "Beloved, now we are the children[13] of God and it does not yet appear what we shall be. But we know, that when it shall appear, we shall be like him; for we shall see him as he is" (1 John 3:2).
>
> "Now the Lord is Spirit; and where the spirit of the Lord is, there is freedom. But we, all with unveiled face beholding as in a glass the radiance of the Lord, are changed into the same image, from one degree of radiance to another, by the Spirit of the Lord" (2 Cor. 3:17,18).
>
> "For God, who commendeth the light to shine out of darkness, has illumined it in our hearts to give the light of the knowledge of the radiance of God in the face of Christ" (2 Cor. 4:6).
>
> "For whom He did foreknow, He also did predestine to be conformed to the image of His Son, that he might be the first-born among many brethren" (Romans 8:29).
>
> "For our conversation[14] is in heaven; from whence also we look for the Savior, the Lord Jesus Christ: Who shall change our vile body, that it may be fashioned like unto His luminous body, according to the working whereby He is able to subdue all things unto himself" (Phil. 3:20).

The idea if the ***adaequatio*** is anticipated in these texts; also a notion of the deeper structure of perception: one ***becomes*** what one perceives, more or less; the more the quality of perceiving is elevated, the more one assimilates oneself.

For modern man and his self-education this means a cultivation of the ***word*** in two directions: the ***perceptual*** world and the world of ***meanings***. In perception, the Logos ***appears*** as the created world: in this sphere one has to increase the receptive attention, by freeing it from the accompanying habitual concepts, which dampen the attention. We encounter ***new ideas*** by schooling our attention for the primal revelation in the sources of ***thinking***, so that the attention can continuously metamorphosize itself for higher levels: from the intentional to the receptive, intuitive attention. In both directions the aim is ***understanding***; this means an approaching of the every-day I towards the true I: in the act of understanding they are united. On the one side, we have a thinking that is independent of language, not abstract, but above all languages, the wordless word; on the other side, we have a feeling structuring — not merely conceptual-nominal — of the perceptual world. Thus the two pendulum swings are united with one another through the impulse of the every-day I, but now no longer on the level of the every-day I. This is the possibility to perceive the ***archetypal phenomenon***; this has no need for intellectual interpretation because it contains its "interpretation" within itself (like the phenomena of

[13] the King James Version reads "sons," whereas it should correctly say "children," as in the Greek, as well as the Standard Revised Version.

[14] King James Version.

the arts as well). This is the possibility for a knowing of the Logos-source, i.e., without the use of sense-organs, but nevertheless a cognition of the sense-perceptible world. Ultimately these ways lead to a creation of a new reality for the future — new heaven, new earth. Then the world will be entering the eighth day of creation; the human being is its creator out of its own initiative and through the spark of the Logos within this beginning. The same path leads also to the realization of the *self-meaning* of the *I*, the human being's eternal name.

What for hierarchical beings is a direct living of one within the other can come about in conversation between human beings through the pendulum swing of the souls. For man, breathing has two pulses: inhaling and exhaling. For angel-beings it is only *one* breath: they *are* God's breath — an exhaling — and this breath is breezing through them, modulated by what is individual within them, which in itself is God's breath. This is possible because they do not have a closed body; they consist in the openness of the forces of the I, like the higher part of man. But in man, this higher I is connected to an enclosed bodily system on the earth; there, God's breath cannot flow through. In the spiritual world, between death and new birth, man is in a certain way an angel-being. There, another kind of breathing takes place: the described breathing in one direction is modified by the separation from the physical body and the preparation for the next incarnation:

> "Regarding our physical language here on earth we mainly experience how we articulate the words on the out-breath. In the life between death and a new birth we perceive that the words which are extended in the universe and whose meaning is the essence of the world and are entering our being on the in-breath of our being, where these words reveal themselves to us as the word of the world. Here on earth we are speaking on the out-breath; in the spiritual world we speak on the in-breath. And by uniting with what the Logos, the Word of the world, is speaking to us, the thoughts of the world are lighting up within ourselves. With our nervous system we make efforts to cultivate the earthly thoughts, but in the spiritual world we inhale the thoughts of the world into ourselves, from the language of the Logos which resounds when we are first spreading our being across the universe."[15]

The song of praise of the angel-beings is their real existence; they have nothing else with which to make music in an earthly fashion. Singing is not a pendulum swing: also human singing is a movement in one direction, an exhaling with a short and brief, if possible unnoticeable in-breath. The song of praise of the angels consists of their allowing God's breath to pass through them, passing it on with their individual participation: this is characteristic of singing. When they are holding it back, not entirely passing it on, they become "fallen angels" who "have lost their beginning" (- *arche* - Jude

[15]R.Steiner, GA 219, 26.XI.1922.

6). Singing is not conversation: when the partners of a conversation are beginning to sing, they sing *one* melody. Question and answer are becoming one. The eye through which you see God is the same eye through which God is seeing you.

The one-beat of existence is described by Dante in the way in which the angel-beings are seeing:

> Queste sustanze, poi che fur gioconde
> de la faccia di Dio, non volser viso
> da essa, da cui nulla si nasconde;
> pero non hanno vedere interciso
> da nova obietto, e pero non bisogna
> rememorar per concetto diviso
> (Paradiso 29:76-81).
>
> And since these substances enjoyed
> the countenance of God, they never turned their glance
> away from him to whom no thing is hidden or unseen.
> Therefore their seeing of new things
> is never interrupted, and no separating concept
> is required for their memory.

God's breath is the Logos: within it no air is necessary to produce the word. The inhaling of the first breath into Adam was the implanting of the spark of the Logos. The second gift of the Logos to mankind is the incarnation of the Logos. This gradually allows the human being to begin its path to becoming a singing, to continue God's breath, the Logos, and to hand on the wind of the spirit in individualized form.

> "If any man speak, let him speak as the word of God; if any man serve, let him do it out of the ability which God giveth...." (1 Pet 4:11).

This is how to understand the word of St. Paul:

> "It is no longer I who lives, but Christ who lives in me" (Gal 2:20).

LOVE AND FEAR

We do not easily understand the language of the Old and New Testament because words which seem familiar to us often refer to ideas we have forgotten or lost. These ideas are not approachable for mirrored thought; they ask for a higher understanding. In this way we also have to look at the fundamental sentence from the *First Letter of St. John* (4:18):

> There is no fear in love, but perfect love casts out fear. For fear is mutilation,[1] and he who fears is not perfected in love.

This sentence can be considered as foundation of a spiritual psychology.

St. John's image of the human being and of the world — they cannot be divided — knows three principles or realities through which the world is constituted, and which are also the essence of the higher — spiritual — man: Primal Beginning, Grace, and Truth — *Arché, Chāris,* and *Alétheia* — in the sequence of their descending rank, *Arché* being the highest.

Alétheia is usually translated as *truth*. But we no longer know the kind of truth which St. John saw; today, we mean "correctness," in the sense that something coincides with something else, e.g., perception with theory. But *A-létheia*[2] means "un-hiddenness," "unconcealed," "not forgotten," "not lost," and corresponds to the living thinking that is experienced within the life and process of thinking, of which only its results, finished *thoughts* and representations appear and become conscious on the level of every-day consciousness; the *process* of thinking happens super-consciously.[3] *Alétheia* is the

---

* Translation: Friedemann Schwarzkopf; from unpublished essay

Kühlewind, Georg. "Liebe und Furcht"

Kühlewind, Georg. *Journal for Anthroposophy*. "Love and Fear." No. 55, Fall 1992. pp. 62-68

[1] "Mutilation:" the Greek work "kolasis" (κόλασισ), which Luther translates as *pain, suffering,* which the Revised Standard version translates as *punishment,* stems from the Greek verb "kolazo" (κολάζω), which originally meant the pruning of superfluous parts of trees and plants. In a metaphorical sense the word means "punishing," "chastising," hence, also "pain."

[2] About the realities of *Alétheia* (αληθεια) and *Chāris* (χαρισ) see:

Kühlewind, Georg. *Becoming Aware of the Logos*. Chap. 10. Great Barrington, Mass.: Lindisfarne Press, 1985.

[3] Kühlewind, Georg. *Stages of Consciousness*. Chap.: "The Two Levels of Consciousness in the Philosophy of Freedom." Great Barrington, Mass.: Lindisfarne Press, 1984.

imaginative thinking, not yet mirrored, reduced, past thinking, representing, or perceiving. We *touch* this super-conscious level of the spirit in every *new* understanding or conceiving of new thought intuitions. *Experiencing* means *remaining*, or staying within this lightning-flash of spirit; this is what is meant by *Alêtheia*. It is no final truth, it is the way and it is life, as experience, from unhiddenness to unhiddenness. "Life" means as much as being present, in the present, and the not-forgetting of the process. *Alêtheia* should be conceived in such a way that the expressions "doing the truth" (John 3:21; 1. John 1:6), "being of the truth" (John 18:37; 1. John 3:19), "knowing that no lie is of the truth" (1. John 2:21) become meaningful.

Love or *Agâpe* (αγαπη) is a feeling-concept for the reality in the world which we call "grace:" *Châris*. *Agâpe*, as the new commandment, is characterized by a "more" in comparison to the old law which says, "love your neighbor as yourself" (Lev 19:18). But the new law says, "love one another even as I have loved you" (John 13:34; 15:12). We hear the same voice in the Sermon on the Mount (Mt. 5; Luke 6) without expectation of reciprocity, without comparison or condition, without self-interest — the death at the cross makes every comparison, every argument impossible and absurd: "love thy enemies." *Châris*, the divine reality pouring over into the world of men is described similarly (Luke 6:32-38): "If you love those who love you, what kind of *Châris** do you have?", etc. The servant who merely does as he is ordered to do is an unworthy servant (Luke 17:9-10).

Châris and *Agâpe* point to an abundance which is naturally given in the divine world; their decreasing means as much as a reduction in the hierarchy of existence. In the world of men, however, *Châris* and *Agâpe* are realities which have to overcome obstacles: obstacles originating in the human being; and through this overcoming, by taking the path through the human being, divine love (the "first" love, Rev. 2:4, 1. John 4:19) turns into earthly love, the "second" love, the ideal of earthly development. Light and love are not an attribute or characteristic of the gods but their form of existence (1. John 1:5; 4:16-17):

> This is the message we have heard from Him and proclaim to you, that God is light and in Him is no darkness.
>
> God is love, and he who abides in love abides in God, and God abides in him. In this is love perfected.

The human being can take part in this divine existence. The ideal of human conduct of life would be: to act only out of the *moral intuition*, the new law, to make it concrete and

*Luther: "What is your *reward*?"
King James Version: "What *thank* have ye?"
Revised Standard Version: "What *credit* is that to you?"
(numbered footnotes by the author, *asterisk*-*-footnotes by the translator)

to adapt it to the needs and circumstances according to ***moral imagination,**** and to manifest it through ***moral technique***. Mankind could live in love: the entire creation of the earth has this purpose, namely, to offer this possibility of a love ***in spite of*** ...., in spite of bodily existence and its requirements which remain unknown to the angels, which the angels are spared.

Divine and human existence are connected through the common principle of "Primal Beginning:" ***Arché***. ***Arché*** is the faculty to create out of nothing, to act without given causes or purposes, the ability to begin or interrupt a chain of causes — for instance, to forgive, or practice mercy instead of revenge. ***Alétheia*** and ***Chãris*** are contained within ***Arché***, as Imagination and Inspiration are contained in Intuition. ***Arché*** is the essential kernel, the star of the human, which ultimately ***remains*** after death, and which strives in the next incarnation to work at the earthly existence, the earthly world, through ***Chãris*** and ***Alétheia***. The forces of growth are concealed within ***Arché*** from where love is out-pouring, from where the light and self-experience of ***Alétheia*** are coming into being. ***A-létheia*** (not-forgetting) has passed through concealment, through forgetting; ***Chãris*** has to become active and penetrate the earthly darkness, penetrate not-understanding; ***Arché*** is absolute being, the ability to grow beyond itself (otherwise it would not be ***beginning***), abundance, as such; ***Chãris*** purely consists of "overflowing."

The faculty of ***beginning*** and growing (or overflowing) is the characteristic — or rather the ***being*** — of I-beings, who are Logos-beings. "In the beginning was the Logos" (John 1:1) as the kernel or driving force of ***Arché***; "was,"** because in creation as well as in human beginning the Logos, the faculty to create meaning and to grasp meaning, must always exist. The past tense form does not allow a temporal interpretation of "primal beginning." Logos is the structuring principle in the world and in man, the predisposition for the ***word:*** the ability to speak, think and love in a human sense (bene velle — to wish the other well). Therefore, the "keeping" or "following" of the logos or the logoi of the Lord (John 14:23-24; 8:5) is the precondition for love of the divine, or identical with it, and thus identical with eternal life (1. John 2:5):

> but whoever keeps his (the Logos') word in him truly, love for God is perfected.

As ***Arché*** is the essence of divine human existence (as it says in the Letter of Jude — Jude 6 — "... the angels that did not keep their own ***Arché***"***), thus the essence of ***Arché***

---

* Moralische Phantasie.

The original Greek uses "was," which is ***im-perfect*, i.e. unfinished, uncompleted past — in contradistinction to perfect, accomplished past: "has been" — which means that beginning in the Logos always ***was***, still ***is***, and continues to ***be***.

Luther translates ***Arché as "principality," the Revised Standard Version as "position," the King James Version as "first estate."

is the Logos. Heraclitus says about it: "The Logos, which is innate to the soul, grows from out of itself."*

The expressions "perfected" (teleiotes), "perfect" (teleios), "to become perfected" (teleioun), "end", but also "fulfillment, completion, culmination, dedication, initiation" (telos), are related in the context of the introductory quotation at the beginning ("*perfect* love:" 1. John 4:18, as also 2:5 and 4:16-17), to the *full* reality of the human being and of the world. The *first* does not exist without the principle of the continuation of creation in the world, and the *last* does not exist and is not fulfilled without the human being's continuation of creation; because within the created world only the human being represents the living Logos. Therefore, one can read in St. Paul's Letter to the Romans (8:19, 22):

> For the creation waits with eager longing for the manifestation of the sons of God. .... Because we know that everything created has been groaning and is still in fear since the beginning until now.

The initiate (the "perfected," teleios) is a human being within whom the original spiritual nature of the *Archê* — and through the *Archê* also *Châris* and *Alêtheia* — can manifest itself *on earth*. The characteristic of *abundance* is described immediately after the Sermon on the Mount, where — after all the unheard-of admonitions (Mt. 5:39) "For if you love those who love you, what reward have you?" (Mt. 5:46) — it says: "You therefore must be perfect ....." In the end the rich youth is told: "If you would be perfect, go, sell what you possess and give to the poor, and you will have treasure in the heavens. ....." (Mt. 19:21).

In Revelations the Logos-Being says: "I am the Alpha and the Omega, the beginning and the completion (Rev. 21:6; 22:13).** And immediately thereafter an example of *Châris* is given (Rev. 21:6): "To the thirsty I will give from the fountain of the water of life *without recompense*."

Perfection is the manifestation of what is predisposed in the *Archê*: the over-abundant, complete love on the level of feeling. Therefore, one can read in St. Paul (Col. 3:14):

> Now draw towards you .... love, above all, which is the bond of perfectedness.

Wherever there is initial beginning, there is love, and without beginning there is no love; and in the primal beginning was the Logos.

The praise of love in St. Paul's First Letter to the Corinthians (Cor 13) culminates in the description of the arrival of the "perfected one." This chapter is the description of the Logos-Being in the light of love. If the human being has no love, it is a plaything of other

*Ψυχησ εστι λογοσ εωυτον αυξων, Heraclitus. In: Kranz, Walther. Ed. *Vorsokratische Denker*. Berlin, Germany: Weidmannsche Verlagsbuchhandlung, 1959. p. 74.

**which is usually translated as "end" (telos).

forces, i.e., it cannot sustain itself as I-being. ***Arché***, ***Chāris*** and ***Alētheia*** are the forms of existence of I-beings: "The I-am is the beginning and the completion" — ***completion*** in the aforementioned sense. These forms of existence mean continuous growing and increasing, and in this sense also: incompletion. This kind of growing, creation out of nothing, is unknown to modern scientific thinking because it looks at the created, the past or result of creation, the world of the laws of preservation of energy and matter.

This increasing or growing can be suppressed in many different ways. Most of the reasons can be found within the human being itself. But if growth is obstructed, this is equivalent to the feeling of fear, the opposite of the spiritual I-am experience, which is realized in growing. Fear is the feeling of "I-am-not:" denied, lacking, and reduced growth. In this sense, fear is mutilation. The I-am lives, exists, ***is*** in ***surrender***, in creating and love. ***Dedication***, receptive attention, the reversed, ***receiving will***,[4] the aim and essence of every meditation, is the possibility for a transformation of the I (or the attention) into ***that*** which the I knows, or ***cognizes***, a transmutation which is experienced. I know ***that*** by experiencing my own metamorphosis into ***that***. For ordinary logic it makes no difference whether one says "I am you" or "You are I." But in reality these are two different movements.

> One can say that, in super-sensible consciousness, the human soul awakens within the spiritual world, but one has to say, at the same time, that ***in the form of love the spiritual awakens within the sense-perceptual world.***[5]

One might compare this statement with the earlier quote of St. John (1. John 1:5; John 4:16).

I cannot transform myself into another I-being because it has no finished existence; it is not merely creature, result, product, but is itself in the process of creating: is a source. One can only change into something that is completed. A formative ***source*** (Gestalt-Quelle), Logos-source, word-source can only be ***received*** into oneself.

In the sense-perceptible physical world, love is the super-natural "law" or commandment. The spirit, if it remains akin to its essential nature, creates something above and beyond Nature when it appears in the sense-perceptual realm. Love is the extinction of one's own I-force by the use of the very same I-force: for the sake of the other. For this to occur the other is needed, and an other exists — in reality — only in the

---

[4]Steiner, Rudolf. ***Vom Menschenrätsel***. "Ausblicke." Dornach, Switzerland: Rudolf Steiner, Verlag, 1957. (GA 20)
Kühlewind, Georg. "The Reversal of the Will and the Encounter with the Logos-force" in ***Schooling of Consciousness***. Trans. et Ed. Friedemann Schwarzkopf. Fair Oaks, CA: Rudolf Steiner College Publications, 1986.

[5] Steiner, Rudolf. ***Die Schwelle der geistige Welt***. "Von dem Ich-Gefühl und der Liebefähigkeit." Dornach, Switzerland: Rudolf Steiner, Verlag, 1972 (GA 17).

sense-perceptual world. The other remains an other also for love — I surrender myself: I become the other by letting him "in." In this way the sense-perceptual world — otherwise completed — gains its perfectedness or wholeness (Heilheit): the power of the continuation of creation enters into the sense-perceptual world through the Logos-force of love. For

> where two or three are gathered in My name, there am I in the midst of them (Mt. 18:20).

In the center of every single human being shines the Logos, and thus also among them. It is the Logos[6] who unites the I-beings.

---

[6]In the Bible — as in every living text — words are never unambiguous, never applied consequently. Whether words such as "Logos" or "Arché" are used in their deepest or in the everyday sense, has to be explored in each case. Often the meaning has to be found on several levels, which gives the text its peculiar coloring. In the profoundest places the words are used in their primal sense which allows for every possible meaning; that is why it cannot be "explained" or defined; it corresponds to the unreduceable original intuition of the respective word.

THE SUPRA-NATIONAL FACULTIES OF THE HUMAN BEING

In almost all countries which have now been liberated from the communist dictatorships, the suppression of their own culture and traditions has created a resurgence of aggressive nationalism. In the age, whose spirit is Michael, this can be considered as a strong adversary impulse, threatening the future which is also dark under other influences. Therefore, it seems to be timely to reconsider those faculties of the human being which are independent of its nationality.

1. In the small child's acquisition of language one can behold two "miracles." One, the direct feeling access to the *meaning* of what is spoken has been described several times.[1] In distinction from the adult, the small child does not reach from the words to the meaning of the sentence (it does not know the words), but through the meaning of the sentence — directly conceived — to the meaning of the words. The second miracle is perhaps still greater: namely, that the child enters the world already *tuned for meaning*, otherwise, the first miracle could not even occur. This being "attuned" is equally as supra-national as the faculty to learn every language that is spoken in the environment of the newly born as its mother tongue, independent of the genetic origin (i.e., genetic descent).

2. Long before verbal communication eye contact begins. This is probably the first communicative gesture between the child and its environment, through the mutually *receptive* (not intentional) look; it is entirely supra-national; likewise, the first smile. After the acquisition of speech, smiling loses its supra-national character because the specific phonetics of the mother tongue influence the movement of the speech organs, and thereby the facial muscles and every bodily movement. By the way of walking and by the gestures, one can recognize the nationality of the human being.

---

* from: Kühlewind, Georg. "Die Übernationalen Fähigkeiten des Menschen." in: *Das Goetheanum — Wochenschrift für Anthroposophie*. Nr. 19, May 10 1992, pp. 199-201. Dornach, Switzerland: Allgemeine Anthroposophische Gesellschaft.

20465 Placer Hills Road, Colfax, California 95713. U.S.A.

24.VIII.1992.

[1] Kühlewind, G..*Das Licht des Wortes*. Kap. 11: "Das wortlose Denken". Verlag Freies Geistesleben, Stuttgart 1984; Kühlewind, G. *Der sprechende Mensch*. Kap.III.2.7: "Das erste Wort." Frankfurt, Germany: V. Klostermann Verlag. 1991.

3. The child receives the first forms of thinking from its mother tongue. As long as the child is thinking in this language, the thinking is entirely corresponding to the spirit of the language. Every language and every language group has its own style of thought which has in the past influenced and determined consciousness.[2] Nowadays, the emancipation of thinking from language normally happens quite early through the encounter with technical and scientific concepts whose expression — the corresponding words — are not given by the mother tongue but are produced by human thought: for instance, paper clip, carburetor, molecules. This emancipation leads towards abstract thought, and in this respect it leads below the level of the mother tongue, because initially these words don't have a feeling-aura, like the words which originally constitute the language. Nevertheless, this development leads to a sort of internationalism. This is like a shadow of the true and real supra-nationality, namely, the possibility to lead the consciousness into levels ***above language*** through the emancipation of thinking from language. This is the possibility offered by meditation because meditation begins with the wordless meaning, of a sentence, for example, and remains within this wordlessness until that which is experienced or observed is articulated.[3] In the language of religion, this means that the Holy Spirit works above language and from the same sphere of consciousness which is also the consciousness level of meditation. The importance of this sphere is often emphasized by Rudolf Steiner:

> If we want to conceive Anthroposophy in the correct sense — from a historical point of view for the present historical moment — it would mean to find an international means for communication across the entire world through which a human being finds the other human being, a means of communication which lies one level higher than language. . . We have to find the way to the spirit of the human being over and above language. . . That means. . . to seek, as it were, for a language of thoughts. The ordinary language of sounds moves in the air and still lives in the sense perceptual sphere. The language which Anthroposophy is striving for will move in the pure element of light — this is meant in more than a pictorial sense — that passes from soul to soul, from heart to heart. And modern civilization will need such an understanding. This will be needed not only for the sphere of higher education, but also for everyday life.[4]

---

[2] Whorf, Benjamin Lee. ***Language, Thought and Reality.*** ed. by John B. Carroll. Cambridge, Mass., USA: The M.I.T. Press. 1956.

[3] Steiner, R. GA 271, 5.-6. Mai 1918;

Kühlewind, G. ***Die Wahrheit Tun***. chapter "Meditation." Stuttgart, Germany: Verlag Freies Geistesleben;

Kühlewind, G. "Die Schulung der Aufmerksamkeit, Kap. Meditation" in: ***Die Freiheit erüben,*** Verlag Freies Geistesleben, Stuttgart. 1988.

Kühlewind, G. ***From Normal to Healthy.*** Chapter "The Path of Knowledge — Meditation." Hudson, NY: The Lindisfarne Press. 1988-1992.

[4] Steiner, Rudolf. GA 307, August 17, 1923 (evening).

4. In our age of individualization, the human being emancipates itself from pre-given group connections. But at the same time a consciousness of ***humanity*** is — or should, or could be — in the process of coming into being which is now uniting all human beings in the sense of Christianity or the Logos. This can be perceived more and more so, even though we are still very far from a ***practical*** solidarity in humanity as a whole. The inhabitants of the earth are becoming aware that their destiny and their interests are common. This unity of mankind would correspond to the Christianity which is not the religion of a people or a race.

5. In the age of the consciousness-soul, the future of the earth is entrusted to the human being. Only the human being can make the bridge across the abyss which separates one from the source of intuition which can give creative impulses for the future. Therefore, human creations are increasingly important — the divine world hardly interferes directly with human history any more, which is different from pre-Christian times. But human creation means freedom, and only in being creative can the human being become free. At the same time the ***true*** individual appears and ***becomes*** through the creation. And everything that is not reducible to causes is new creation; therefore "creation" means not only works of art or new thoughts, but also many inconspicuous gestures such as intuitions of a pedagogue or the act of forgiving, i.e., everything that comes about out of nothing (even though under specific circumstances), as a ***beginning,***[5] within which the Logos is active.

Through creative activity in the aforementioned sense, the superconscious[6] part of the human soul, its spiritual part, is individualized from below in the same way that self-consciousness begins with the feeling of the body, "the own-life of the spirit within itself,"[7] with the everyday-I or ego.

The greater these creations are, the more individual they are. And the more they are individual, the more they are universal; i.e., they address many human beings, in principle everyone, supra-nationally.

6. It is a central thesis of Thomas Aquinas that there is something in the world that is universally addressing humanity independent of language and nationality. The doctrine of universals says that (1) in the individual objects, the human being can recognize, or at least touch, only these universals, namely, the ***being*** of the individual things (essence),

[5] Kühlewind, G. ***Die Erneuerung des Heiligen Geistes.*** Chapter "Der Logos im Seelenbereich." Stuttgart, Germany: Verlag Freies Geistesleben. 1992.

[6] Kühlewind, G. ***The Life of the Soul Between Subconsciousness and Supraconsciousness.*** Chapters 1 and 3. Hudson, NY.: The Lindisfarne Press. 1990.

[7] Steiner's expression for the soul in general, in his work ***Theosophy.***

and (2) *only the human being* is able to recognize this essence — in principle; that is the hope. ***Universalia*** therefore means two things: on the one hand, the common constitutive nature of individual things, for instance, the idea of "lionness" in every single lion; and secondly, the word means that this essence, the ideas of things, is accessible to every human being, even if not actually but at least as a possibility, and is therefore "universal" also in this sense. The ability of the cognizing human soul to *touch* the universals — at least or even to conceive them, to cognize their Being — demonstrates the spiritual nature of the soul. This is what allows the human being its *infinite* development. Thus, Thomas says,

> anima intellectiva, quia est universalium comprehensiva, habet virtutem ad infinita.
>
> because the soul is able to conceive the universal, therefore the spiritual soul has the potential for the infinite.[8]

7. One who is able to understand universals also has the faculty to produce them: this happens with human creations; they are universals and in principle they are accessible to every human being — at least at the age of the consciousness-soul. We can appreciate the art of many cultures and epochs, and at this stage our European culture is also becoming universal (for example, nowadays one finds musicians from almost all nations who *understand* how to play Beethoven or Mozart). The lowest class of universals are concepts: even these are already supra-national, even though in the abstract sense. But the example of J. S. Bach shows clearly the paradoxical phenomenon that he is a representative of Baroque *and* German music, but at the same time extremely individual. The individuality of his music does not disturb either the German or the Baroque character. On the contrary, less important composers are less Baroque and less German. The more a work is inspired by the Spirit of the Times, the more the folk-spirit, and that which is entirely individual comes to appearance. If one wants to find the folk-spirit today one has to depart from the level of the Spirit of the Times, i.e., from above. The human being connects initially with the Spirit of the Times and in doing so it unites the folk-spirit with the Spirit of the Times; as a source of inspiration this would be primary today, otherwise the result can be the destructive nationalism of our time. Today, the universal-spiritual is the signature of the Spirit of the Times, Michael, and at the same time of the truth of Christianity, understood as Logos teaching and Logos realization.

8. The emancipation of thinking from the mother tongue in the age of the consciousness-soul is decisive for the realization of a supra-national consciousness of mankind. This is a possibility because the folk-spirit works the strongest in languages. As this effect is generally missing today, there would remain the inheritance of the soul-body

[8]Summa Theologiae I, 76: 5 ad 4.

or sensitive body which used to mediate the family- and national-character by being permeated by the sentient soul (see: *Theosophy,* "Re-embodiment of the Spirit and Destiny"). But even the sentient soul has nowadays become largely independent from the folk-spirit because of the emancipation of thinking; on the other hand, an inheritance of the soul-body which would be adequate for the folk-spirit is hardly possible any more because of the intermixing of peoples. This phenomenon serves the individualization of the spirit, and today, for instance, it would be entirely out of time to try to imitate on the scale of a people such as the Jewish, customs of Old Testamentary times regarding the purity of the line of inheritance, which was actual at those times. In the story of Ruth one also sees that in certain cases foreign blood has been admitted even into the most important line of inheritance: the lineage of Solomon, the origin of Jesus.

Today nationalism has a similar role in the community of peoples, which is represented by egoism in the individual, for instance in the economic sphere — both are entirely and altogether out of time in the age of the Spirit. Wordless meditative thinking would be humanity's way out of the risk. In that sense, Steiner says:

> and therefore it is the case that Michael is strongly rejecting everything that is separating, for instance, the separation by the human languages. As long as one is only enclothing one's cognitions in the words of languages, not elevating them to understanding thinking, one will not reach the proximity of Michael. Therefore, we also have a quite significant conflict in the spiritual sphere today. On the one hand, the Michael impulse has just entered the development of mankind: now is its time. But on the other hand, there is much within the development of mankind that it simply does not want to accept, which wants to reject this Michael impulse. And that which wants to reject just this Michael impulse is also, for instance, the feeling of nationality which flared up in the nineteenth century and became stronger in the twentieth century, and continues to flare up more and more. According to the principle of nationality, much has been brought not into order but into disorder in recent times. It has really been "misordered."
>
> All of this is, in the most terrible sense, in opposition to the Michael principle. All of this contains Ahrimanic forces which are in opposition to the entering of the impulse of the Michaelic forces into the earthly life of the human being. And there one sees today this conflict between Ahrimanic spirits storming upwards, which want to carry upwards that which surfaces from the inherited impulses of nationality, something that Michael is strongly rejecting.
>
> Today we have, in fact, in this direction, the most vehement spiritual battle because the habit is spreading across a large part of humanity that there are not thoughts, but that people are thinking in words. But to think in words in this way is not the way to Michael. One only comes to Michael if one penetrates through the words to true inner spiritual experiences if one does not cling to the words but reaches true inner spiritual experiences. This in fact is the mystery of modern initiation to reach beyond the words to the experience of what is spiritual. This is nothing that would contradict a feeling for the beauty of language especially because when one is no longer thinking in the language, only then one begins to

develop a feeling for the language to stream as an element of feeling within and from the language. But that is something for which human beings must first strive.[9]

[9] Steiner, R. GA 233a, January 13, 1924.

BEHOLD, I MAKE EVERYTHING ANEW

The Resistance

A healthy life of consciousness would have the inclination to improvise: always dissolving what is already given and achieved. The experiences that are already made are not forgotten — the "laws" are not annihilated through the New Testament — but the new approach rests not on the *results* of the past, but on *faculties* which arose from experience. For instance, the adult does not remember how, as a child, he learned to read and write the individual letters, but he *can* read and write. "Moral intuition" means a faculty of improvisation in the discovery of what is "here and now" *moral*, a faculty which has absorbed the old moral laws as well as conscience, so that these can respond to the needs of a particular situation. Against such a development, tremendous resistance comes up within the soul, in the individual as well as in the collective.

Seen from without, these resistances are the reflection of a convenient habit and of fear; fear is perhaps the primary one. Fear arises when the egoity is threatened with losing its outer supports, and when it is not yet strong enough to maintain its inner uprightness without these supports.

Language and the conceptual system that it supplies — later even the abstract conceptual system which is independent of any language — are initially "standing in" for man's individual form of I-being: it is their role to support the I until it is able to make out of the given preliminary forms its own entirely sculptable form, which corresponds more to its improvising nature. When the path of the soul is not leading towards this goal, every "dissolution" is threatening with the loss of the conceptual order and arrangement of the world — the *given* — threatening that the supports of the I would fall away. The result is fear. Trying to help itself, the I attempts to master the new experiences with already acquired, *given** concepts, with the result that the essential aspect of such new experiences is normally rejected. And this is feeding the tendency to link the surety of judgment — with respect to truth, goodness and beauty — to outer attributes: how can

---

* from: Kühlewind, G., "Siehe, ich mache alles neu", in: "Das Goetheanum", 66. Jahrgang Nr. 22, 24. Mai 1987, Dornach, Switzerland; translated by Friedemann Schwarzkopf, 20465 Placer Hills Road, Colfax, California 95713.

* *Italics* = emphasis by the translator; E x p a n d e d text = emphasis of the author.

one come to true "statements," logical judgments? Such questions marked the philosophical research of the last decades, and even before. This supported the tendency to formalize thinking in order to guarantee its "correctness." The attempt was made to create an unambiguous language. We know that these attempts failed as a result of inner contradictions. But in the process the greatest paradox was not even noticed: that the regulation of thinking has to occur through a thinking that is not yet regulated, and that the creation of an unambiguous language is already requiring the existence of such unambiguous language in order to agree upon the necessary conventions. If these attempts were successful, they would prevent the creation of new conceptualities or new logical developments, and thus once and forever determine an inner and outer "world." Simply speaking — more on the psychological level — this attitude is characteristic of the need for authority.

All varieties of "applied" soul-gestures — in contra-distinction from the "improvising" ones — tend to seek security in outer, i.e., sense-perceptible, attributes because the *source* of surety, the *feeling of evidence*, on which logic is founded — or the feeling for beauty in the aesthetic realm — is not noticed, or is forgotten. When the cognitive feeling cannot orient itself by ideas, the feeling component of the cognitive activity separates from the process of understanding, and becomes — in this independence — a "mixed sphere" in the experience, consisting of self-feeling and a kind of "intuitive" feeling, always more or less colored by the egoity. Therefore, the expectation for "feeling" — for knowledge saturated with feeling — arises in the one who tries to grasp the new phenomenon by using old conceptualities because the inadequate concepts are not connected with the higher feelings. Thus the feeling-life is separated from the life of ideas; it is also anticipated in a different sphere. This becomes the incubator of non-cognitive, subjective feelings.

It cannot be denied that languages with their d e f i n e d words are supporting the inclination towards convenience in the life of consciousness, since one can r e m e m b e r the appearing signs — one has to — instead of having to create the signs and meanings intuitively anew. The more the appearing signs are becoming independent, the more man is subject to this passivity because the corresponding inner activity is continuously weakening. If one is spiritually striving, one should try to fight against this tendency; the first step in this direction is the achievement of thinking a statement or sentence in a w o r d l e s s manner, which is the beginning or precondition of meditation. The conscious avoidance of generalizing, classifying pseudo-thinking — originating in remembered contents — with regard to spiritual and psychological phenomena is the beginning of this battle.

The Signs

Surety in cognition, in the aesthetic and moral life, cannot be found in the sense-perceptible sphere because this appears separated from the intuitive thinking. It is convincingly demonstrated by the more recent theory of science that the sense-perceptible sphere does not even "exist" without conceptualities; therefore, cognitive surety cannot be gained, because one cannot examine "every case" empirically, and because the thinking is supposed to be reliable only in formal disciplines like logic or mathematics. Thus empiricism is limited to sense data; however, it is not noticed that the sense-data are not *given* without conceptualities, even if these conceptualities are of a higher kind.

The search for surety in the "sign" — the perceptual given — is caused by the insecurity of thinking with respect to itself. This insecurity is self-annihilating because it is only thinking that determines and assumes such insecurity. Its real reason is the fact that — at the present stage of the structure of the consciousness-soul — only thought becomes conscious, whereas its source, the *process* of thinking, is not witnessed because it has shifted to the super-conscious sphere. *Witnessing* would give such security; but without such experience, only the *feeling of evidence* remains as the inner norm of thinking, which is indeed unsure because it is intermingled with non-cognitive feelings.

The insecurity in thinking could only be removed through a willed and conscious education of the imaginative or living thinking. It is within man's *freedom* to begin his path in this direction. Thus his choice can also take the opposite direction: a regressive path in the expectation that security is g i v e n, through a "safe" theory or teaching, an authority, similar to the way in which concepts were given in the past: *together with* their processes and perception simultaneous w i t h the corresponding concepts. Therefore, one could tend to look for an "unfailing" authority, which is never allowed to be wrong; this would imply an unfailing judgment of the followers of such an authority because they identified it, determined and postulated its unfailingness. This is the convenient path, which wants to spare inner activity, although the experience demonstrates that it is not so easy to "think" even a simple concept, and that such a concept is only experienced, if it lights up — like a "gift" as it were — from the plane where this surety originates. This plane would have to be consciously experienced, if one wants to find surety.

The search for *signs* really means that one is looking for *mechanisms*. But "signs" are only for the one who takes them as "signs", i.e., as indication for one's inner supplementing activity. What is expected are just such percepts, which would deliver surety in the respective field, at the same time sparing this inner activity. This gesture is often described in the New Testament. On the one hand, the Pharisees are expecting signs in order to identify the individuality of the Lord; yet those signs which are given, are interpreted as coming from the devil and considered as invalid "There shall no sign be given unto this generation (Matthew 12: 38-39; Mark 8: 11-12; Luke 11:29; John 2:18)." This characterizes the decision about those who are looking for signs because they would not want to ***understand*** such signs; they do not really want signs, but an altogether given security.

The New

The fact that man is able to produce new ideas, works of art and new moral impulses, leads to his connection with the creative principle of the world — the Logos — which is always accessible. When the Word-being within the human being begins to be effective and to come to expression, the continuation of the creation of the world is possible; this is the only source or seed-point for the future. This corresponds to a metamorphosis within the human being itself, when the direction and orientation of life passes over from natural man — the bodies, i.e., from the physical-, life-, and soul-body — to the ***upper***, spiritual man, who consists of the free forces around the true center of the I. Within the ***natural*** man these forces have adopted forms and have gone through a process of formation. But at this turning-point the nous pathetikos — as characterized by Aristotle — is received from the hands of the creational powers and brought under the control of the nous poietikos, the poetic, creative human being.

The expression of the "new creation" appears in the letters of St. Paul (2. Corinthian 5:17):

> "Therefore if any man be in Christ, it is new creation (or: he is a new creature); old things are passed away; behold, all things become new."

The last sentence is a direct reference to Rev. 21:5, the title of this chapter.

What this "being in Christ" means, is expressed in the preceding verse (2. Cor. 5:16): "Wherefore henceforth know we no man after the flesh..." Likewise, in the letter to the Romans (8:1): "There is therefore now no condemnation to them which are in Christ Jesus, who walk not after the flesh, but after the Spirit." This shift of the pivotal point of life from the bodily to the spiritual aspect is also strongly emphasized in the letter to the Galatians, where the expression "new creation" appears in a similar reference (Gal. 6:14-15).

The story of the "Manna" (Exodus 16:8-36) is a parable about the impossibility of conserving or even "having" Spirit or "spiritual contents;" these must always be renewed, newly "collected." Otherwise they turn into poison that stops the life of the Spirit in its improvising nature which is always newly creating. In this sense we can read (Exodus 16:16-20):

> This is the thing which the Lord hath commanded: "Gather of it every man, according to his eating, an omer for every man, according to the number of your persons; take ye every man for them which are in his tents." And the children of Israel did so, and gathered, some more, some less. And when they did mete it with an omer, he that gathered little had no lack; they gathered every man according to his eating. And Moses said, "Let no man leave of it till the morning." Notwithstanding they hearkened not unto Moses; but some of them left of it until the morning , and it bred worms, and stank: and Moses was wroth with them.

There is no "having" in the soul-spiritual sphere; neither a "calling upon" something that belongs to the past, whether events, or principles. For in the sphere of the present— which is not "past"— there is no "something". The proceeds or results of a faculty must not be confounded with the faculty itself; and on the plane of life there are only faculties. The "yesterday" is allowed to continue only in the form of a faculty.

Thus, the being-on-this-level consists in the continuous renunciation of what is "just-achieved," the continuous overcoming of the "having-found," continuous becoming. He who "has," "has found," who is not renouncing, falls out of this sphere. To be in poverty, to remain "poor," is the only way to remain. For poverty alone has the power to attract the Always-New.

THEORIES OF CONSCIOUSNESS*

Ladies and gentlemen, I don't know how long you will agree with me tonight, but I am sure that you are agreeing in the beginning, when I am saying that thinking is a dangerous undertaking because thought always is dangerous for the dictatorial systems, and for the thinkers, too. But I think — you remember Socrates — that it is the most dangerous undertaking to think against current thinking modes; and that is more dangerous than anything, at least in Europe.** I don't know how it is here. I will try it. To mitigate a possible conflict, I tried to pack my poisoned arrows in some kind of humor. You can already guess that from the seven titles of my talk, which will be presented in seven parts.

1. Don Quixote — Sancho Panza

I will begin with the first phenomenon — and I have already mentioned it this morning — that we have a technology based on natural science, and we have a philosophy which states that one cannot find certainty in the world of perception by means of inductive methods. I would like to make this clear for everybody. I read it in a book about this subject. You all know the metal "copper," and you know that copper is a good conductor of electricity. Now, according to philosophy you cannot be quite sure — never — that every piece of copper is a good conductor of electricity because you cannot make experiments with all pieces of copper. You may have a cellar underneath with — maybe — a piece of copper that doesn't conduct electricity — because we don't know. We must always try to make an experiment. Being a natural scientist, I dealt a lot with physical chemistry. If I think now of any theory of metals, of conductors, then I would say that this means, in other words, that not every piece of copper is copper. But that wouldn't convince a philosopher. Now we have this problem that philosophy,

* lecture Tuesday, April 22, 1986, 8.00 P.M.
University of California Los Angeles (UCLA)
Sponsor: International College
Transcript: Susan McManamon, Edited by Friedemann Schwarzkopf.

** In 1986 Hungary still had censorship of publications.

epistemology, states that you cannot be sure by inductive methods, and technology is based on the absolute certainty that every piece of copper is a good conductor of electricity. The funny thing is that the success and the justification of natural science as "science" doesn't come from philosophy, it comes from technology, from the success of technology. I think many of you know that, epistemologically, natural science is not very well founded, not even founded at all, because the fundamental concepts are very unclear. For instance, Newton introduced that "power" equals "mass" multiplied by "acceleration:" P = M x A. This acceleration contains "space" and "time;" these four fundamental concepts are not defined, not even described. This equation defines them in a circular mode. That's where the problems arise. I choose to call this problem *Don Quixote*. You know this figure which is a very "realistic," very "practical" person. Now, our ***Sancho Panza*** is the Technology and our Don Quixote is the Philosophy, the Epistemology. They work somehow together but in such a manner that Sancho Panza doesn't care about Don Quixote.

I would like to take this as our departure point, because you can ask, "Why is that so?" This is very interesting because philosophy states that we can have certainty in the field of logic, and in the field of mathematics, but not in the field of the perceptual world; you can ask, "Why is that so?" The answer of philosophy is, as far as I know, and perhaps somebody can correct me if I am not quite right, that in logic and mathematics we have something that is very hard to define. It is ***understanding***. Do you "understand?" In the perceptual world, as epistemology states it, we have ***no*** such understanding, such, I would say, self-conscious understanding; we must always support ourselves on perception and therefore there is something that doesn't exist. Now, here begins our problem: In the perceptual world there seems to be no such understanding as in logic or mathematics or geometry. And indeed there is a problem. There are two problems, but now I would mention only one. The first reason why there is no such understanding is because, according to most of our consciousness-theories, there is nobody who could understand.

2. Odysseus

This "nobody" leads us to our second point, which is named "Odysseus," and if you know the story of the Iliad, then you can understand why this chapter is named "Odysseus." After he blinded the one-eyed giant Polyphemos, this Polyphemos asked for his name, and he was sly enough to tell him "I am nobody." That helped him very much because the giant wanted to call the other giants for help, and they asked him "Who hurt you?" and he said "Nobody." So this "Nobody" is the second item that we have to deal with.

If you are investigating the current theories of knowledge about cognition and consciousness, even in psychology it is very hard to find that there are two items missing. One missing item is the mentioned "understanding;" I would say "linguistics," the concept, or idea — or whatever you call it — of "understanding." And the second is the subject of who understands. These two are missing.

Therefore, we have a general problem, and I would say: What a miracle that we have ***certainty*** in logic and mathematics, because there seems to be somebody who ***understands***. Even if it is not clear who that funny person is, or subject, or thinker, or understander, but there is ***understanding***, at least.

Now, I don't know if you are aware that you already made a vote by coming into this room and by sitting here. And this vote was discovered by a German philosopher, Karl Otto Apel. He is now living somewhere in Germany. And he discovered that if people come together to discuss, or to have a conversation, they make an hypothesis — not consciously. You might make the supposition that you come here and listen to me: "Maybe it has sense. I am not quite sure that it hasn't any sense." And that means that you are supposing that — now I quote Apel, but not in his words (Most of you wouldn't understand his language; not that he speaks German, but he speaks a special philosophical language which one must first study.) — that we are "I-beings," egos, whatever that is, and that we have cognition, that cognition is possible, that knowing is possible, that communication is possible between us without limits. I won't dwell on this. You can easily show that if you suppose that there are limits in communication, then communication doesn't come about, not even to the limit. That was your vote when you entered this room. Were you conscious about that? Or are there perhaps individuals sitting here in the audience, who think that an "I-being" doesn't exist? Such a thing like a human ego that cannot be reduced to something else — it doesn't exist? This is a funny thing because if I would tell you now that "I am not existing," I think you would laugh, or take it as a joke — in the best case. But if I am making a very earnest fact, telling you that a human subject is nothing else than . . .; and here you can substitute something, but not human subject, human "I-being" or "ego being," something else: the brain mechanism, or heart mechanism, or kidney mechanism, whatever you want but not an "I–being" — that is an entity that cannot be reduced to something that is not being. Then it may be that you would say, well, this man is very erudite, he knows something, he is a scientist.

That is the only difference: that one speaks in the first person or the third person. If I am saying: "I am not," then you laugh; but in the third person it can be a scientific statement.

Mostly we speak in science as if we would not exist. There cannot be found a responsible personality about which somebody is saying something. We are so used to that, that if I am telling you this, you can perhaps say, "How is that possible?" You cannot find in science the responsible person, the responsible source that sponsors what is said. I know one philosopher in Austria, Hans Jonas, who deals with this problem. But it is very seldom that you find even the question clearly articulated. There must be somebody who is staying behind our statements, who is responsible for what he is stating, and this is very hard to find. One makes every possible effort to reduce this somebody to entities which one has discovered. It is one of the problems a theory of consciousness must avoid. The first thing is who is speaking. ***I*** am telling ***you*** something. The ***author*** is telling something ***to the reader***. He tells something and "you understand," "you know what I mean." Well, if you understand this question, then you ***are,*** too. To make the statement "I am not and you are not," that is funny and you can't do it that way, that would be a joke. But the same statement in the third person is possible. There is "nobody" speaking, that is his ***name*** .

3. The Pot

Now we will speak about reduction. One has tried to reduce not only the "I-being," the ego, to something else, but other activities of the human mind as well: for instance, thinking. This reduction is impossible, the reduction of human intelligence to something that is not intelligent: mechanisms, natural processes and so on. The reduction of consciousness to unconscious elements that are discovered and dealt with by the consciousness, originates somehow from sub- or unconscious elements. This circularity is never allowed in other sciences but in the science of consciousness; in the statements about consciousness, it is.

What I am saying here is not new. Most of these seven points are not new, not at all. Perhaps they were not seen together, in their interdependence, complexity and meaning. Perhaps that is what I am trying to do. The single items are not new. For instance, there are a lot of thinkers who discovered this fact that, if you are reducing human intelligence to something that is not intelligent, then your statement is suspended; e.g., if you are saying, "Thinking is a perfectly determined process." And this last sentence was also determined by some mechanism in your brain or in your stomach or whatever. That is clear. For instance, David Bohm in his book "Chaos and Order," he is perfectly aware that this is not possible because these statements are "hanging themselves" (i.e., executing themselves), self-suspending. After having discovered that — three pages later — he makes the same mistake in reducing human intelligence to something that is not intelligent.

You see, there are statements that are not possible. One of these statements is well known, that of the "Cretan Liar:" "Every Cretan is lying;" and this statement is made by a Cretan. Now you have the problem that this is more than 2000 years old. I won't dwell on the possible solutions supplied or offered by philosophy during these 2000 years. I would only say, if a Cretan could say, "Every Cretan is telling the truth," then nothing catastrophic would occur. It is not possible to say, "Now I am lying." You feel that this is not possible — in this moment — but it is possible to say, "Now I am not lying." You have no problems with that.

But with this example I want to refute certain solutions proposed to this problem. For instance: "Cognition is not possible" from an agnostic point of view — except for *this* cognition, the understanding of this postulate?! Do you see the paradox?

So you have here something that I called the "pot" and I will tell you why. Because, if I tell you that there is *no* cognition, then I put all possible "noise" into the pot, but I have forgotten my statement. My statement is the *handle* of the pot. Very few pots have the handle inside the pot. You are holding the pot always from the *outside*. You forget the handle because you have it in your hands. But the handle is always used earnestly: if I am saying: "There is no cognition", then *this* cognition doesn't count! There are a lot of examples. I can give you hundreds of such statements that are "pot" statements, that are "handle" statements of pots. But if you would be consistent you could not have made this statement.

For instance: There is someone in Germany who made the following statement: "There is no such thing as *evidence*." Evidence is the inner norm of thinking — thinking in a logical way. If you ask, "How do you know that you are thinking logically?" you cannot take refuge to books, books about logic, because if you cannot think logically, you cannot learn that from books. You don't understand the books if you cannot think logically. So sometimes it is very hard to understand these books (not to mention the author who couldn't have learned his logical thinking from the book he was about to write). You can quote only the written books. It is very difficult to quote the unwritten books.

Now, this man speaks about "evidence."

But first I must tell you a story. I was interested in evidence, and in my younger years I expected some substantial thinking behind it, and I asked a famous mathematician, "Tell me, what is the mathematical evidence that you are so often referring to in your books?" Well, he was embarrassed, too; then he told me, "Well, that is a feeling." *A feeling* ? Yes, it is a feeling. You cannot do anything about that. You feel; "*thus* it is logical — *this way* is not." You can make mistakes in that way, but in the same way you can also *correct* the mistakes. There is a Latin saying, "Errare humanum est" — "To err is human." And that is said always with a negative connotation, but I think that it is very positive. You know why? Because a deterministic system cannot make errors and if it could, it could not discover these errors. "Error" is always a *discovered* error. The possibility to make errors in thinking or in cognizing means that we are *free* in this field, otherwise it would be impossible to discover the error.

Coming back to the statement that there is no such thing as evidence: If he wouldn't continue the sentence I would think, "Well, it is a statement." But the sentence is continued, and how do you think it continues? "There is no such thing as evidence, *because...*" Now, you see the difference: "*because...*" what is that? He appeals to evidence, to my feeling that I will accept his argument by feeling that it is evident, that there is no such thing as evidence. That is what happens. He didn't recognize the *handle* of the pot. I could call this "the big forgetting;" forgetting what I am doing behind my deed, forgetting my statement behind the content of the statement. If the content would be true, I could not have made this statement. These are the structures that are repeated and you can find these structures of thinking repeatedly in many theories of consciousness. But "consciousness" is perhaps too narrow a term.

Another problem of this sort is that most models of consciousness are constructed in such a manner that — if they would be realistic, if they would be true — the model couldn't come about. How do you know that? If a theory of consciousness is not applicable to itself, then it is a very dangerous theory. For instance, you have a great blooming of behavioristic theories. If you ask, could these theories come about if their content would be correct? — please think about that — I think that is not possible. You couldn't account for the origin, for the coming about of these theories, if the content were correct. That is also a common feature of many theories. Try to apply it to the theory itself — there must be a consistent possibility to apply the theory: *that* is "the handle of the pot." The theory consists of many statements which, if the theory would be right, could not come about, because it is in contradiction with the activity that has produced the theory. For instance, the statement, "There is no evidence;" how can we prove it? We must always take recourse to evidence. "There is no argument." Another example: "There cannot be certainty in cognition, surety of cognition." There are very refined thinkers who say, "Well you are right, this is not sure, this is only a belief, that is not a cognition, only an opinion, a belief, or something like that." He thinks now, poor fellow, that he has saved himself. I am not so easily convinced, because now I try to discern what he said: "That it is only a belief;" is that certain, or uncertain? You cannot escape from this because the last sentence is always taken very earnestly. That is always the "handle of the pot." Some pots have handles that are reaching very high — long handles. You cannot make negative statements about that which you are doing; that's the expression in the field of consciousness.

So, that is "the pot." It has also a lot of implications but I think you can feel this kind of circularity.

4. The Illiterate

The next section is called "The Illiterate" because it refers to nominalism. Nominalism is the statement that words are the same as concepts, and that there are things without concepts; they are only names. You put only "name-tags" on the things that exist, without any conceptual limits. But you can only give a name to something that is already a "something:" ***That*** you can question only with respect to something that is already ***something***, already a "what." ***What is that? That*** must be very clearly outlined, selectively contoured; you can distinguish ***that*** from its surroundings, and you can do that repeatedly. These two features, selectivity and repeatability, make the conceptual character; there is already "something" — something that was forgotten for reasons which we cannot analyze here. I will give you an example where the conceptual aspect of our perceptual world is quite clear. It is a very practical example about the so-called "perceiving" of robots. I hope you read science fiction. In science fiction novels you always find these robots to be very intelligent and especially able to perceive very well. That means they can recognize their "master" and the "wife of the master," and so on. They are perceive perfectly, like human beings. That is really fiction, and it is fiction for the following reason: because robots have no concepts. For example, I have a very intelligent robot, and now I want to teach him that this is a "bag." Now I put this bag into the focus of the robot's camera and I write, "bag." The problem is this: now I an wearing ***this*** suit, and tomorrow I can wear a black or a dark suit, and I must teach the robot anew because it cannot separate this bag from the background. It "sees" it together with the background. Therefore, if I want the robot to recognize this bag, I have to show it to him in front of all possible backgrounds. And then there is the following step because the bag can be shown in different perspectives. It is an entirely different form; and then I can turn it, and show it from below, from the side, diagonally, etc. What does that mean? I have to make millions of pictures, and even then it wouldn't be certain that the robot would recognize this bag in a certain, unforeseen situation.

What is the problem? If you have a little boy or girl, you show him or her what a bag is. Once this is understood, this child recognizes the bag in every situation, in every hand, in front of every background, and so on. And not even ***this*** bag but this other bag, too — you see this is quite another bag but the child would say, "that is a bag, too," and if you had a red bag or a yellow bag, it doesn't matter; or if the bag is a bit smaller or bigger, and so on. That is the concept — this child has a concept, ***understanding***; and that is the problem of our robots. Only in very special situations they can be trained to "recognize."

Now, why is this called "The Illiterate"? I must again come back to the computer story because there are two ways to deal with a page of a *text*.

One possibility is this: You can make an exact equation, not a mathematical description of where the black and white spots are on this page — you can do that perfectly. In Zürich, I heard a professor of computer science who taught: to understand a piece of music means that you can make a program that reproduces this music. That means that the person who can make this program need not even know that these are notes. He need not hear ***music***. It is not necessary that he has any musical experience. He can make the program perfectly without knowing that his program deals with notes. This is the way an illiterate would deal with a text. He would make equations, or measure the distances of the letters of the lines, measure the angles of the lines that make up the letters, and so on.

But the other possibility is that we can ***read***. If we can read the text, we make quite another gesture in our consciousness — we don't care about the size and distances and angles, or the frequency of the letters. You would not be able to reproduce or draw the letter "G" in a book which you have recently read. You don't remember. Why? Because you are absolutely not interested in the form, you are interested in the content.

5. The "Flat" Fly

Reading and calculating — these are two absolutely different gestures. In *reading* you must "read together." You are not interested in the letters, not even the words. You are interested in *meaning*. You must create this meaning. It is not given. If you are not attentive, you don't catch the meaning. You catch the words perhaps. There is the possibility that you have a sentence in a philosophical text where you "understand" every word but not the sentence. Now, this *reading* is a very important concept.

When we are reading *words*, we are not on the level of the letters, and in reading sentences, we are not on the level of the words. We are always ascending to a higher plane. You cannot assemble letters to a word if you are on the level of letters. You must always have a distance to the letters and then you can have the word. And so it is with sentences, too. Likewise, if you have a paragraph you must read together all the sentences that are contained in it. You must go above the level of the sentences. If it is a really important book, then you must read it together with all other important books that exist, because — in a funny way — they relate to each other. You won't quite understand modern philosophy without the surrounding philosophies and the philosophies of the past. You must "read-together."

There are many ways of reading: simple reading and higher reading and this gesture of "reading-together" is quite a different gesture from calculation. You can calculate the black and white spots on a page, but that's not reading. Therefore, the title of this section is: "The Flat Fly." That is the law of *levels*. This is formulated in mathematical language by *Goedel* (for the mathematicians in the audience). He formulated for the field of mathematics the concept that you can't understand something on the level where it is.

I will give you another example which is more philosophical. There was a philosopher in Göttingen, Germany. In the twenty's of this century he wrote a very famous essay which proved that epistemology cannot exist. It was very simple: because you use the same "cognizing" which you want to describe in your theory, it cannot exist. I would say he is somehow quite right. This story of epistemology shows that he even had the experience that it isn't possible, and he looked for the reasons. He gave the reasons quite well, but the background of these reasons is that we have a consciousness (or an intelligence) that has only *one* level.

But the question is — the supposition is not clearly spelled out — has human consciousness only one level of cognition, one level of intelligence? Is that true? Is it true that it cannot be developed any further? That is the question.

"The Flat Fly" is a discovery of Einstein. He used the picture to show that a flat fly cannot discover the third dimension. He was not right. You know why? Because a really flat fly cannot discover the second dimension. To discover the two dimensional surface it must be above the surface, a little bit, to look at it, or else it would not discover it. And that is why I have chosen this title. He wasn't quite right, Einstein. To discover two dimensions there must be a fly that is not altogether flat. But the principle of levels of reading is already there. You can see that clearly if you observe how the little child learns to read: to read letters, then to read words, then to read sentences; this is a catastrophe for the consciousness, it must begin a new reading at every stage.

6. The Bucket or "The Bag"

Now, "The Bucket" is in honor of Karl Popper, his famous essay, "Bucket of..." The "bag," that is empiricism. Empiricism is always the empiricism of sense perception, and it has a tragic story. First mankind thought, "Well that is very simple, let's observe; don't bother with theories, they will come; we must observe." That is very easy to say, but it is not easy to do, because we must know ***what*** to observe. We cannot observe everything. If I would observe everything — sitting in this chair — I would observe for a whole lifetime, only this part of the world which I am now seeing: the first row of seats. There is a lot to observe. There are so many details I would not even come to the second row. Therefore, in scientific observation, you need a selection. One can see this well in the history of physics: once Galileo had given the conceptual framework, people knew what to observe. Thus they could observe, make experiments, and so on. There is always a theory behind observing; you must know ***what*** to observe, not everything, not every detail. You must know: "this is the essence I have to observe." For instance, the ***velocity*** of a falling stone — that's not natural yet it is natural for us that a stone is falling.

Now, the other problem is to distinguish between what originates in perception and what comes from thinking. That is a great problem; that is the problem of the ***given*** as perception. Because if you are investigating that, you come to very surprising discoveries.

For instance, you begin with a reflection. In the moment of reflection we have in the perceptual sphere a lot of singular distinct entities, without relation, without connection. But if you ask, "How do I know where such an entity ends?" Like the robot "knows" where the bag ends? — it cannot know. Only if you have the concept: then you know, otherwise not. Therefore, in order to have structure in the perceptual world, structured into distinguishable units, entities — whatever — you already need the concepts. This was discovered very early.

And if you are radical, you eliminate from this given perceptual world all concepts, one after another; then the last concept that will remain is: "There is a *difference*." And if you eliminate *this*, then you have a continuum that is not structured. That is the *directly given*, without any structure.

That is not a normal human experience. A human experience that comes close to this is described in the experience of Kaspar Hauser. I won't dwell on that — you know the story. There we have an example how the world would look without concepts, or almost without concepts.

Descartes knew that the perceptual world is structured with concepts — much more than we imagine. Then Hume discovered that ***causality*** doesn't originate in perception. Kant discovered that ***space*** and ***time*** come from the human source, not from the perceptual world, and today this is continued by the positivists, phenomenologists, etc. And today we know that even the slightest structure in the perceptual world, which can be repeatedly experienced, has conceptual nature.

7. Uroboros

The conclusion is this: Where, within the "given," can we find a point to rely on which is pure empiricism.* The perceptual world does not provide this point because it is a continuum when we eliminate all concepts. But thinking is given, and thinking in its "givenness" is clear to us; that is, if I really *think* something, I don't need an explanation. You can't give explanations to ***my*** thinking. Not that it is impossible but it is not necessary — you can ***say*** something you didn't understand, but you cannot ***think*** something you don't understand. Here we have a point: and this point is that empiricism is perhaps possible with regard to thinking itself. Pure empiricism: I would say: naive realism (with regard to thinking); you can take thinking as it is. You cannot make any other gesture. Any other gesture would be an "a posteriori" description of what you do (when you are thinking); grammar, for instance. Grammar isn't a prescriptive science. It *describes* what we do. We are used to speaking English. Then the grammatist comes and describes that. How? The little child speaks much better English than a philologist

* Empiricism means the principle that we establish our knowing on *experience,* initially sense-perceptual experience and, in the second step, experience of the reality of the cognitive movement itself.

or a linguist, who may be French for instance, or Hungarian. This child does not know that grammar exists. It knows nothing. Then science, grammar, linguistics and phonology describe what we do; logic likewise. Logic is an "a posteriori" description: "thus we are used to thinking." Logic is never exhaustive because I can make *new* gestures — at every moment. Logic is always a description of what is *already thought*.

But there is the following possibility: This possibility is the symbol of the snake which holds its tail in its fangs. In Greek it is called "Uroboros." It is an *ancient* symbol.**

You see, we have thinking as given. In this point we can rely on empiricism. We, people of modern times — since the time of Renaissance — can *reflect* on consciousness. We can reflect on thinking. We can manage to "think about thinking" but *that* is not very fruitful. Because it remains on the *same* level; therefore you can't really get insights about thinking.

But we mentioned the *feeling of evidence* that rules our thinking — if we are *really* thinking. This is at the boundary of our consciousness — it is the boundary we *feel*. But perhaps this boundary can be extended, as Heraclitus said it in his time: "The boundaries of the soul can never be explored because they are expanding with every wondering about them."

And now I want to give you an example of such a boundary experience. I am an experimental person. I don't like theory. I won't give you a theory of consciousness. I am saying that you can have the *experience*. I would say, by way of experience you can build up an empirical science, but this empiricism does not relate to the perceptual world — because we saw that it is fully imbued with concepts — it relates to thinking. This is not possible without *schooling* and training of consciousness. Today, many thinkers feel that something has to happen in this field, and we have a great spectrum of propositions suggesting how it can be done. At this point we have no time to go into these diverse propositions, nor to distinguish the best way, or why I am choosing this option (of schooling). We cannot do that. But there is the possibility, and I would like to make an attempt to show you that it is not impossible.

** The gesture of the Uroboros asks us to direct our attention at its source. In that way attention is at the same time creating a state of concentration while simultaneously beholding concentratedness

The question of where we find the experience (empiricism) of the unifying gesture of the Uroboros leads us to our attention. Attention is not given, we ourselves have to give it. Initially, attention needs a theme to be given in order to be able to focus. In that way not-given and given are united as expressed by the image of the snake that holds its own tail between the fangs. In that sense, the translation of the image of the Uroboros would be "only attention can behold itself." (Annotation by translator)

Because of that, it is not very often that we have *new* ideas. Do you know that? May I ask you, when was the last time that you had a *new* idea? But now, if you have a new idea, then even if it becomes very clearly conscious to you, you must put it in words. You must formulate it, otherwise it remains only a "lightning," I would say a "feeling," but even to yourself it is not clear. You must formulate it. Then you have to make a sentence. To make a sentence you have to choose the first word, the second word, the third, and so on. How can you choose that, if you don't know *what* you are formulating. This "what" is not yet clear, not yet consciously clear. But it is there, otherwise you would not be able to put the sentence together, the words. You must know how you do that. The "what" is there, even if it is not clearly conscious. It can occur to you, but it is *super-conscious,* it is at the boundary of consciousness: I would say the "feet" of this new idea are already "dangling" somewhere at the head-level. But to be conscious of it, you need to formulate it.

And then it can happen that you are not content, not satisfied with this formulation and you say, "well this formulation does not quite correspond to my idea." And at this moment you are comparing the words, the formulated words, with *what?* With something that is not at all clearly conscious, but is present in such a strong manner that you can make the comparison!

With these thoughts I only wanted to show that this possibility — to extend the consciousness in the direction of where our experiences of evidence are originating — is not out of reach. Instead of "theories" of consciousness I would suggest an experimental way, or an *empirical* way because we do not *have* "knowledge" about consciousness: ***consciousness is ability*** It is a *faculty,* the ability to think, ability to speak, without theories, without knowing how — we don't know *how* to speak. Not even the mechanism of uttering sounds is conscious, neither is grammar to the little child. You can study the grammar of your mother tongue; well, you can study that, but I don't think you speak according to your studies. You are speaking according to your first genial acquiring of language in a consciousness that psychology describes only by taking refuge in a consciousness common with the speaking environment. You can see that today, too — for instance, the last time I read in the book of Merleau-Ponty about the "Primacy of Perception," there was a very fine chapter about this — otherwise you cannot explain that a little child acquires language and the ability to think without *having* language and thinking. There is a recourse to a more or less "common" consciousness in which there is naturally another problem that arises — it is not noticed in these psychologies of the child

— it is that this "common consciousness" has no physical support as there is no common physical brain.

So, here we are; thank you very much for your attention.

Questions and Answers

Q: Why did the Buddha say in the heart sutra: "There is no cognition"?

A. That was a provocation. If you understand this statement, it is more than any theory. There are a lot of such statements, for instance, in Zen-Buddhism. You always find: "You have no Buddha-nature." But if you ***understand*** this sentence, you are activated in your Buddha nature. Absolutely, that is there. Today we have a lot of such provocations, but we take the provocations earnestly. We could turn them into *koans*: "You are only a lot of atoms, of molecules. You know? You understand?" "There is no understanding, you understand?" These provocations could be used as koans. Therefore I think that it was a Koan: "There is no cognition." Koans do not theorize, they give possibilities to *experience* what cognition is, by saying: "There is *no* cognition."

Q. I have a two-part question. You seem to be suggesting in this discourse, that an epistemological theory would not end in words, is that correct? The question is: if we are going away from the level of words, how can we make our epistemology in words?

A. If you have an *experience*, or, I would say, a great *intuition*, you can always find the *form* to express it. If you have a new idea, you have put it into old words. You don't invent a word. You put it in old words. There is the possibility to make such attempts to express even these cognitions or experiences which are made on a higher level.

Q. Then the appearance of the validity of the text could not come from the words or the intrinsic logic in the text itself? Is that right? Does the person reading the text have to have access to the *experience*?

A. This is the case with every demanding text. If you have a "text," it is always telling you as much as you are understanding. It cannot tell you anything else. If it is a trivial text then you have no problem. In a newspaper, I think we don't have great problems of cognition: "What does this text tell us?" But if you are reading philosophy or some other demanding text, say the sermons of Buddha, then you have to be *active,* otherwise you will only have the surface. These texts, like the sermon of the Buddha, or the sermons of the Gospels have a lot of levels of meaning, innumerable levels. You can go and go and go, but a text cannot tell you anything more than what you understand. Thus, my speaking transforms into that which you understand, or in the extreme case you would say, "I don't understand anything."

Q. "The Flat Fly:" If the "flat fly" has to have attributes already of the three-dimensional realm to have any understanding of the dimensional realm, I would carry this on to the human being. Then you seem to imply, that we — in order to understand the consciousness of the three-dimensional world — have to be in a further dimension. In that sense, the theories which we make about these realms must be "postscripts" which are made after we have left the realm to which they apply.

A. Yes, that is absolutely so, and the whole history of epistemology is a confirmation of that. And the break-down of "demanding" epistemologies happens because of this reason.

Q. So you have led us into the fourth dimension tonight?

A. We are always there, when we are ***understanding.*** We are not understanding in the third dimension. But we don't notice that, we only take short sips of these realms, like a frog takes air when he comes to the surface of the water.

BIBLIOGRAPHY

WORKS BY GEORG KÜHLEWIND

BOOKS IN ENGLISH

Kühlewind, Georg. *Stages of Consciousness — Meditations on The Boundaries of the Soul.* Trans. Maria St. Goar. Eds. Christopher Bamford, Fred Paddock. West Stockbridge, Massachusetts (now: Hudson, N.Y.): The Lindisfarne Press. 1984.

Kühlewind, Georg. *Becoming Aware of the Logos — The Way of St. John the Evangelist.* Trans. F. and J. Schwarzkopf, ed. Ch. Bamford. West Stockbridge, Massachusetts (now: Hudson, N.Y.): The Lindisfarne Press. 1985.

Kühlewind, Georg. *From Normal To Healthy — Paths to the Liberation of Consciousness.* Trans. Michael Lipson. Great Barrington, Massachusetts (now: Hudson, N.Y): The Lindisfarne Press. 1988.

Kühlewind, Georg. *The Life of the Soul between Subconsciousness and Supraconsciousness.* Trans. Michael Lipson. Hudson, New York: Lindisfarne Press. 1989.

Kühlewind, Georg. *The Logos-Structure of the World*, Trans. Friedemann Schwarzkopf. Hudson, N.Y.: The Lindisfarne Press, 1992.

Kühlewind, Georg. *Working with Anthroposophy — The Practice of Thinking.* Hudson, New York: Anthroposophic Press 1992.

COLLECTED ESSAYS

Kühlewind, G. *Schooling of Consciousness.* Translated and edited by Friedemann Schwarzkopf. Fair Oaks, California: Rudolf Steiner College Press, 1986.

Kühlewind, G. *Thinking of the Heart.* Translated and edited by Friedemann Schwarzkopf. Fair Oaks, California: Rudolf Steiner College Press. 1987.

Kühlewind, Georg. *Feeling Knowing: Collected Essays.* Translated and edited by Friedemann Schwarzkopf. Fair Oaks, California: Rudolf Steiner College Press. 1994.

ABOUT GEORG KÜHLEWIND

Schwarzkopf, Friedemann. *The Metamorphosis of the Given — Towards an Ecology of Consciousness — Empirical Idealism as Foundation for Paradigmatic Thinking (Also Under Consideration of J. W. Goethe, R. Steiner, and G. Kühlewind).* Dissertation. San Diego, California: American Commonwealth University, 1992. Ann Arbor, Michigan: U.M.I. University Microfilms Intl. 1992. Catalog: LDO 2454.